God bless

W. Perryman

St John 8:32

The Drama of Obama on Racism

Analyzing Obama's Speech on Race

Rev. Wayne Perryman

BOOK PUBLISHERS NETWORK

Book Publishers Network
P.O. Box 2256
Bothell • WA • 98041
PH • 425-483-3040
www.bookpublishersnetwork.com

10 9 8 7 6 5 4 3 2 1

Printed in Canada

LCCN 2008930067
ISBN10 1-887542-85-x
ISBN13 978-1-887542-85-2

Proofreader: Julie Scandora
Typographer: Stephanie Martindale

*You shall know the truth
and the truth shall set you free.*

John 8:32

About the Author

As a former newspaper publisher and radio talk show host and in his current profession as a political consultant and a fact-finding investigator in discrimination cases for the plaintiff, Rev. Perryman devotes much of his time serving his church and the inner-city community. As a respected leader in the black community, he has received both recognition and commendations for his ongoing humanitarian work, including commendations from former President George Bush Sr. (Republican), the United States Congress (members of both parties), former Washington State Governor, Booth Gardner (Democrat), and former Mayor of Seattle, Charles Royer (Democrat).

In addition to this recognition, Perryman's work with children, gang members, professional athletes, and major corporations has resulted in local, national, and international media coverage. Among them include: C-Span Book T.V., Fox's Hannity & Colmes Show, *Sports Illustrated*, *Parade*, *Sports Illustrated for Kids*, the *Seattle Times*, the *Seattle Post Intelligencer*, *Ebony*, *Upscale*, *EM*, *Christianity Today*,

Charisma, the *Personnel Administrator*, *The Economist*, ABC's Home Show, TBN, the 700 Club, and Italy's *Speak Up Magazine*.

As a renowned researcher and fact-finding investigator, Perryman's work has won the respect of our nation's top scholars. In 1993, Rev. Perryman challenged major Christian publishers with his book entitled: *The 1993 Trial on the Curse of Ham*. In this explosive research book, he proved that the publishers were wrong when they published books and materials which stated, that according to the Bible, *"the black race was cursed."* For over five hundred years the curse theory was used to justify slavery, establish Jim Crow laws, and promote racial inferiority and superiority. Based on Perryman's research and recommendations, two major Christian publishers and the *Encyclopedia Britannica* made the decision to remove this false theology from several of their publications (see Appendix D).

CONTENTS

An Analysis of Obama's Speech on Race

As an independent voter and a fact-finding investigator, I was asked to review and analyze Obama's inspirational and fascinating speech on race. Many believe it is one of the best speeches since Dr. King's *"I Have a Dream"* speech, and I agree. But I have one problem. He missed the opportunity to set the record straight on two issues that he brought up during his speech.

1. His first missed opportunity came one minute and thirty-four seconds into his speech, when he referred to the Declaration of Independence and how it was ***"stained by this nation's original sin of slavery..."***

Although he follows up and talks about how slavery ***"divided the Colonies and brought the convention to a stalemate,"*** he failed to point out that **as a nation** we were always divided over the issue of slavery from the time the first slave ship arrived in Jamestown, Virginia, in **1619**, to the end of the Civil War **246** years later.

He should have told the audience, that there has ***never*** been a universal endorsement of slavery by the ***white citizens*** of this country and that ***white America*** has always been split over the issue of slavery. He could have mentioned that **175** years before the Emancipation Proclamation was signed, the Mennonite Quakers (white folks) of Germantown, Pennsylvania, passed an ***anti-slavery*** resolution in **1688**. It was the first formal protest against slavery in the Western Hemisphere. Under this resolution, Quakers who participated in the slave trade were threatened with expulsion.

He should have mentioned that in **1711**, sixty-five years before the Declaration of Independence was signed, our **white founding fathers** passed colonial legislation to outlaw slavery, but their law was overturned by the British Crown.

He should have said the issue of slavery was so divisive that white churches split, white families split (some fighting for the Union and others for the Confederacy) and eventually our nation split, which resulted in the Civil War.

In proving that our **"nation"** (meaning all of white America) never really endorsed slavery, he should have told his listening audience that by **1835** the anti-slavery movement had over 435,000 members and these ***white abolitionists*** fought and gave their lives to express their opposition to slavery and the mistreatment of African Americans.

By failing to point out the massive number of whites who not only opposed slavery but literally gave their lives to end it and racism, he merely perpetuated the myth and lie that our **nation** (implying that every white in America) endorsed or approved of slavery and Jim Crow. He should have made it clear, that it wasn't ***every white***—it was primarily the white supporters of the Democratic Party—the party that became known as the ***Party of White Supremacy***.

2. His second missed opportunity came twenty-one minutes and fourteen seconds into his speech when he made the following reference to slavery, Jim Crow, and the anger of his pastor:

- *We do not need to recite here the history of racial injustice in this country. But we do need to remind ourselves that so many of the disparities that exist in the African-American community today can be directly traced to inequalities passed on from an earlier generation that suffered under the brutal legacy of slavery and Jim Crow....*

- *...The anger is real; it is powerful; and to simply wish it away, to condemn it without <u>understanding its roots</u>, only serves to widen the chasm of misunderstanding that exist between the races....*

In order to foster a better understanding of the *roots of racism,* Obama should have told his audience that the <u>roots of racism rested in the soil of the Democratic Party</u>, not in our nation as a whole.

He should have informed Americans that without the political backing of those who made up and formed the powerful **Democratic Party** (a party whose members gave their lives and spent billions to preserve the institution of slavery and the system of Jim Crow), slavery would have ended one hundred years earlier, and Jim Crow would have died in the womb of those who conceived it. Contrary to public opinion, racism **was not** something that the entire white race engaged in. Racism was the political agenda of a powerful political party – made up of individuals who chose to use this deadly disease to cover their own insecurities in their relentless quest for wealth and power. The following facts, are facts that the Senator chose not to use regarding the role his party played in establishing racism in America.

1787
Democrats Attempt to Use Slaves to Gain Power

During the Constitutional Convention in 1787, the pro-slavery members (who eventually became the Democratic Party five years later) argued that slaves should be counted as citizens when considering the number of congressional seats their state would receive. They made this argument even though they had no intentions of giving the slaves the same rights afforded to the white citizens of their states. The anti-slavery members (who eventually became the Republican Party) strongly opposed this racist proposal. To finalize the Constitution and not give in totally to the pro-slavery members, they reached a compromise with a three-fifths clause. Under the new clause, the pro-slavery states could only count the slaves as three-fifths of a person when determining how many congressional seats their state would receive.

Shortly after this matter was settled, Pierce Butler, a representative from the slave state of South Carolina argued that the document should include a Fugitive Slave Clause. Under his proposed recommendation, runaway slaves would be classified as criminals and treated as such. To avoid any further delays in finalizing the Constitution, the Constitutional Convention approved the clause but stated the federal government would not enforce this clause - enforcement would be the responsibility of the individual slave state.

1793
Democrats Pass First Fugitive Slave Law

Six years later (1793) and one year after the formation of the Democratic Party (1792), Democrats introduced the Fugitive Slave Law of 1793. This law included a clause to impose fines on anyone (abolitionist) interfering with the slave master's right to re-claim his slave. Northern states countered by passing Personal Liberty Laws to protect free blacks from being kidnapped or mistaken as slaves. The Democrats were furious.

1819
Democrats Gain Another Slave State

When Missouri petitioned to join the union, the pro-slavery Democrats rushed to make it a slave state. Their goal was to expand slavery and gain a majority in Congress. A compromise was reached when Maine applied for statehood. The *Missouri Compromise* as it came to be known permitted Missouri to join the union as a slave state and Maine as a free state.

1844
Democratic Platform Supporting Slavery

In 1844, the Democratic Party stated the following in their 1844 Platform: *"Congress has no power to interfere with or control the domestic institutions of the several States; and that such states are the sole and proper judges of everything pertaining to their own affairs.... That **all efforts by the abolitionist and others, made to induce Congress to interfere with questions of slavery**... are calculated to lead to the most alarming and dangerous consequences."*

1850
Democrats Modify Slave Fugitive Law

Pro-slavery Democrats fought for and passed a modified version of the Fugitive Slave Law of 1793. Under the new modified law, slaves weren't permitted to testify on their behalf, and federal commissioners would be assigned to every county in the country to conduct hearings. These commissioners received $5 if they decided that the black person on trial was not a slave and $10 if they decided that he was a slave. Under this new law some nine hundred slaves were returned to their master. Democrats claimed that over eleven thousand had escaped between 1850 and 1861 (Boyer 2001, 317).

1852
Democrats' Platform Support
New Fugitive Slave Laws

After the passage of the modified <u>Fugitive Slave Law,</u> the Democratic Party stated the following in its <u>1852 Platform:</u> *"Resolved: That the foregoing proposition covers and was intended to embrace the whole subject of **slavery** agitation in Congress; and therefore the **Democratic Party** of the Union, standing on this national platform, will abide by and adhere to a faithful execution of the acts known as the compromise measures and the acts for **reclaiming fugitives** from service or labor. The **Democratic Party will resist** all attempts at renewing in Congress or out of it, the agitation of the slavery question, under whatever shape or color the attempt is made."*

1852
Horrors of Slavery Revealed in New Book

In 1852, Harriet Beecher Stowe released *Uncle Tom's Cabin*, exposing the horrors of the institution of slavery, the institution that the Democrats swore to protect and defend in their 1852 Platform. Stowe sold three hundred thousand copies and reignited the abolitionist movement to end slavery.

The Institution of slavery was established, supported and protected by the Democratic Party -as stated in their political platforms.

1854
Republican Party Formed to End Slavery

In 1854, the anti-slavery members of the Democratic Party joined forces with the Abolitionists and formed a new political party. They called themselves the Republican Party. Their primary goal and mission was to end slavery and give blacks the same rights afforded to white citizens.

1854-55
Democrats' Efforts to Make Kansas a Slave State

Believing and hoping that Kansas would become a slave state, Democratic President Franklin Pierce, pushed through the Kansas Nebraska Act, a law that would allow the individual states to decide whether they would be a slave state or a free state. The pro-slavery Democrats sent hundreds of individuals to Kansas and succeeded in fixing elections and forming a pro-slavery legislature. The new pro-slavery government passed laws to execute anyone who assisted runaway slaves. Republicans and Abolitionists countered and formed their own anti-slavery government. The two opposing governments fought for control of Kansas.

1856
Republican Senator Beaten for Speech on Slavery

One year following the passage of the Kansas Nebraska Act (1856), the struggle between the anti-slavery and pro-slavery forces intensified when pro-slavery forces (representing the Democratic Party) invaded Lawrence, Kansas. It was reported that as many as two hundred persons were killed during the invasion. The act of terror would be known as "*bleeding*

Kansas." When news reached Congress, Republican Senator Charles Sumner took to the Senate floor and delivered a fiery anti-slavery speech. The speech infuriated Democratic Representative Preston Brooks of South Carolina. While Sumner was yet speaking, Brooks took a walking cane and attacked the Senator, nearly beating him to death. The attack resulted in an all out fist fight between Democrats and Republicans. In his book, *Charles Sumner*, Professor David H. Donald of Harvard gave the following account of what happened after the dust settled:

While Brooks was being led off, Sumner, partially supported by Morgan, lay at the side of the center aisle, his feet in the aisle, and he leaning partially against a chair. He remained senseless as a corpse for several minutes, his head bleeding copiously from the frightful wounds, and the blood saturating his clothes. Dr. Cornelius Boyle, who had been hastily summoned, dressed the wounds, which were still bleeding profusely, and put two stitches in each. Sumner's shirt around the neck and collar was soaked with blood. The waistcoat had many marks of blood upon it; also the trousers. The broadcloth coat was covered with blood on the shoulders so thickly that the blood had soaked through the cloth even through the padding and appeared on the inside; there was also a great deal of blood on the back of the coat and its sides. [At the hospital] Before falling into a daze sleep Summer remarked: "I could not believe that a thing like this was possible."

Arrested on a charge of assault, Brooks was immediately freed under a $500 bail, and became the hero of the extreme pro-slavery clique. Armed and menacing, Southern fire-eaters [Democrats] *talked of imitating Brook's example, and made violent threats against other Northern leaders.* [Saying] *"It would not take much to have the throats of every Abolitionist cut. If the northern men had stood up, the city would now*

*float with blood. And if Congress dared to discuss Brooks'
actions, the House of Representatives would ring vollies* [sic]
from revolvers" (Donald 1996, 282-298).

1856
Democrats' Response to Beating
of Senator Sumner

After the savage beating, the Democratic Party published the
following in their 1856 Platform: *"Resolved: That we reiterate
with **renewed energy** of purpose the well considered declaration
of former Conventions upon the sectional issue of Domestic
Slavery and concerning the reserved rights of the States."*

1857
Democrats Pleased with
the Dred Scott Decision

The Democratic Party rejoiced when the United States
Supreme Court overturned a lower court's decision in the case
of *Scott v. Sandford*, better known as the ***Dred Scott Decision***.
In a 7-to-2 decision, the court decided that the African slave
was not a citizen of the United States but the mere *"**property**"*
of his owner. According to *The Oxford Companion to the
Supreme Court of the United States*, the opinion of the Court
was shaped by a variety of factors. The most obvious was
*"the attitudes of the individual justices toward the race
problem."* The *Oxford Companion* reported that by 1837, of
the nine justices, *"**five of them were Democrats appointed**
by President Andrew Jackson: Roger Taney, John McClean,
Henry Baldwin, James M. Wayne and Philip P. Barbour. The
other four members of the court, including Taney were from
slaveholding states, while only one, McLean, could reasonable
be suspected of harboring anti-slavery leanings"* (pp. 237

and 810). On page 925, *The Companion* goes on to state that *"From 1790 to 1861 (with the exception of a few years in the early 1830's), the majority of the Supreme Court justices were Southerners. In addition, __most of the Northerners on the Court were Democrats who voted with their pro-slavery southern colleagues__."* (*The Oxford Companion to the Supreme Court of the United States* is the collective work of over 350 legal scholars, both Democrat and Republican).

1860
Democrats React to Republican Victory

In 1860, the anti-slavery Republican Party won its first election and President Lincoln became the first Republican President of the United States. Democrats were angry, particularly southern Democrats. In an act of rebellion, the Democratic state of South Carolina seceded from the Union, while other Democrats made threats to assassinate the new anti-slavery President.

1860
Democratic Political Platform on Fugitive Slave Law

In 1860, the Democrats' 1860 Platform included the following statement: *"Resolved: That the enactments of the State Legislatures to __defeat the faithful execution of the Fugitive Slave Law are hostile in character, subversive of the Constitution, and revolutionary in their effect__.*

1861
Democrats Leave the Union
and Launch Terrorist Attack

By February of 1861, six other slaveholding Democratic states followed South Carolina and seceded from the union. Soon after they adopted their own provisional constitution and formed the new Confederate States of America (Witcover 2003, 213). Two months later, on April 12, 1861, the Confederate military launched a terrorist attack on Fort Sumter, and this was the beginning of the Civil War.

1862
Democrats Angered over Emancipation
Proclamation

As the Commander and Chief of the United States Armed Forces, President Lincoln issued the Emancipation Proclamation freeing all slaves in the rebellious states effective January 1, 1863. The Proclamation angered Democrats and made them more determined to win the war.

1864
Democrats Oppose the 13th Amendment

In 1864, Lincoln was re-elected, and a Republican dominated Congress passed the 13th Amendment to *free all slaves and abolish slavery in the United States and its territories*. The **northern Democrats that remained in Congress fought hard to defeat this and other Civil Rights bills**. Speaking for the Democratic Party, Fernando Wood of New York argued: *"The proposed Amendment to abolish slavery in the states of the Union is unjust, a breach of good faith and utterly irreconcilable.... It involves the extermination of all white men of the southern States and forfeiture of all the land*

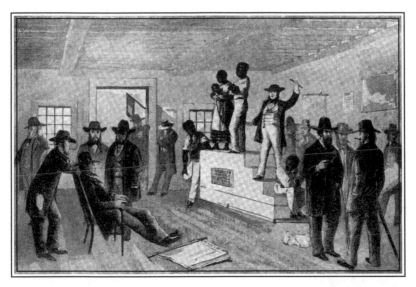

Under slavery and Jim Crow, the two institutions supported by the Democratic Party, the lives of millions of blacks were destroyed."

and other property belonging to them. Negroes and military colonist will take the place of the race [that will] *be blotted out of existence."*

1865
Democrat's Support of
Slavery Kills Millions of Blacks

The end of the Civil War meant the end of the Democrats' institution of slavery. It was an institution that had brutally murdered and destroyed the lives of **million of blacks**. Historian, John Hope Franklin said, *"It has been estimated that 900,000 slaves were imported in the 16th century, 2.75 million in the 17th century, seven million in the 18th century and four million in the 19th.... When one considers the many recruits who must have been killed while resisting capture and the vast numbers who died during the Middle Passage, together with the millions who were successfully brought to the Americas, the aggregate approaches a staggering figure.. Whether the figure is 15 million or 50 million, it is a grim testimonial to the fabulous profits that were realized, the ruthlessness with which the trader operated, and the great demand for slaves* (Franklin 1973, 19). As of this date (June 2008), the Democratic Party has yet to offer a public apology for supporting and maintaining this inhumane institution of human bondage and for its racist system of Jim Crow.

1865
President Re-Elected and Assassinated

In 1865, President Lincoln was re-elected. During his second Inaugural Address on March 4, 1865, Lincoln talked about the two political parties. He said, *"Both parties deprecated war, but one of them would make war rather than let the nation survive and the other would accept war rather than to let it perish* (Hunt 1997, 200). One month later he was assassinated by Democrat loyalist, John Wilkes Booth.

1865
Republican General Gives
Blacks Forty Acres and a Mule

Four months before the assassination (January 16, 1865), Union General, William Sherman initiated the first Reparation program for African Americans when he issued Special Field Order #15. Under the order, each black family would receive forty acres and a mule to work the land. Republicans also established the Freedmen's Bureau of 1865 to support General Sherman's efforts.

1865
Democrats Introduce Black Codes

Southern Democrats responded by passing the Black Codes of 1865. The Codes virtually re-enslaved the African American. Under the Codes blacks were suppressed, restricted, and denied the same constitutional rights and privileges afforded to their white counterparts (Ploski and Williams 1989, 137). The Codes established whom African Americans could or could not work for, the type of employment they could pursue, evening curfews, and restrictions on travel. Many blacks were forced to work for their former slave masters as apprentices.

1865
Northern Democrats Re-Assure
Southern Brethren

After the war ended, Northern Democrats re-assured their southern brethren that they had supported the war to preserve the union only, not to give blacks equal rights with whites.

Northern Democrats were quoted as saying, they agreed *"to sacrifice life and limb in the defense of the Constitution and the Union, but not for the **nigger**"* (Witcover 2003, 228).

1866
Democrats Oppose Reparation Bill for Blacks

In February 1866, General Sherman's field order (which gave blacks forty acres and a mule) was introduced into Congress as a new bill, <u>Senate Bill 60</u>. Although the bill passed the Republican dominated congress, the new Democratic President, Andrew Johnson, vetoed the bill, forcing blacks to return the 40 acres to their former slave owners.

1866
Democrats Oppose the 1866 Civil Rights Act

In 1866, Republican Senator, Lyman Trumbull of Illinois, introduced the <u>1866 Civil Rights Act</u>. The new law challenged the southern Democrats' Black Codes by *declaring that all persons born in the United States were now citizens, without regard to race, color, or previous condition. As citizens they could make and enforce contracts, sue and be sued, give evidence in court, and inherit, purchase, lease, sell, hold, and convey real and personal property. Persons who denied these rights to former slaves were guilty of a misdemeanor and upon conviction faced a fine not exceeding $1,000, or imprisonment not exceeding one year, or both.*

Northern Democrats argued against the passage of this law. Reverdy Johnson, a **Democrat from Maine** argued that the law could not apply to blacks because: *"The Supreme Court had already ruled in the Dred Scott case that a person of African descent, whether born free or whether free by birth or free by after events, is not, within the meaning of* *the Constitution of the United States, a citizen."* He went on to state that under this law the black man would have *"the same right to enter into contract of marriage with a white woman as a white man has..."*

William Saulsbury, another **northern Democrat from Delaware** argued, *"I regard this bill as one of the most dangerous that was ever introduced into the Senate of the United States..."* Democratic President Andrew Johnson vetoed this bill, but the Republican Congress overrode his veto.

1866
Democrats Oppose the Freedmen Extension Act

To strengthen their previous legislation, Republicans passed the Freedmen Bureau Extension Act of 1866 to extend the life of the Freedmen Bureau. Again, President Johnson gave his support to the Democratic Party and vetoed this bill. The defiant Republican Congress over-rode his veto.

1866
Democrats Oppose the 14th Amendment

Republicans introduced the 14th Amendment to give blacks citizenship. **Northern Democrats** fought for two years (from July 16, 1866, to July 28, 1868) to defeat this bill. Congressman Andrew Rogers, a **northern Democrat from New Jersey** argued that the proposed Amendment was: *"An attempt to in-graft upon the Constitution of the United States one of the most dangerous, most wicked, most intolerant and most outrageous propositions ever introduced into this house."* He went on to say, *"I have no fault to find with the colored race. I wish them well, and if I were in a State where they exist in large numbers I would vote to give them every right enjoyed by white people except the right of a Negro man to marry a* *white woman and the right to vote. God save the people of the South from degradation by which they would be obliged to go to the polls and vote side by side with the Negro."*

1867
Democrats Oppose Reconstruction Act

In 1867, the First Reconstruction Act of 1867 was passed. The purpose of this Republican sponsored legislation was to assign military officers to oversee the Reconstruction of the South by setting up government systems to assure equality. Again, Democratic President Andrew Johnson attempted to veto the law, but the Republican Congress overrode his veto. Professor John Hope Franklin reported that: *"When southern whites* [Democrats] *had almost complete charge of Reconstruction, a kind of guerrilla warfare was carried out against both blacks and whites who represented the Washington government in the South. It looked as though the Civil War would break out anew as **Democrats resorted** to every possible device to overthrow the radicals* [Republicans]" (Franklin and Moss 1998, 226-234).

1868
Democrats' Platform Fears Negro Supremacy

The Democratic Platform of 1868 called for: **"The abolition of the Freedman's Bureau and all political instrumentalities designed to secure Negro Supremacy."** The Platform also praised Andrew Johnson for his consistent attempts to veto key pieces of civil rights legislation. The Platform stated: *"We do declare and resolve that the President of the Untied States, Andrew Johnson, in exercising the power of his high office in resisting the aggression of Congress upon the Constitutional rights of the States and the people, is entitled to the gratitude of the whole American people; and in behalf* *of the **Democratic Party**, we tender him our thanks for his patriotic efforts in that regards."*

1868
Democrats Expel Blacks from Georgia Legislature

In 1868, Georgia Democrats publicly stated that the Negro is *"unfit to rule the state"* and further stated that they would protect their Negroes but *"would not let them be governors, congressmen or judges"* nor could they [Democrats] ever *"elevate an inferior race over a superior race."* After making this statement, with the use of violence, they expelled all of the black elected officials from the Georgia legislature.

1868
Democrats Call Republicans "Nigger Lovers"

During the 1868 Presidential race, the Democratic national party referred to Republicans as *"Nigger Lovers"* and displayed large campaign posters which said: *"This is a white man's country – Let the white men rule."* Their actions and attitudes toward blacks earned them the proud title of: ***The Party of White Supremacy***.

1869
Democrats Oppose the 15ᵗʰ Amendment

In 1869, Republicans sponsored and introduced the <u>15th Amendment</u> to give blacks the Constitutional right to vote. In arguing against this, bill Thomas Hendricks, a **northern Democrat from Indiana** said: *"I do not believe that the Negro race and the white race can mingle in the exercise of political power and bring good results to society. We are of different races. Men may argue about it as much as* *they please; we know that in many respects there is a great difference between the races. There is a difference not only in their physical appearance and conformation, but there is a difference morally and intellectually and I do not believe that the two races can mingle successfully in the management of the government. I do not believe that they will add to the common intelligence of the country when we make them voters...."*

A Democrat from Mississippi later said: *"I am just as opposed to the Negro educator, Booker T. Washington as a voter, with all his Anglo-Saxon re-enforcements as I am the coconut-headed, chocolate-colored, typical little coon, Andy Dotson, who blacks my shoes every morning"* (Franklin 1973, 59).

1870
Democrats Oppose the
Enforcement Act of 1870

In 1870, Republicans introduced the <u>Enforcement Act of 1870</u> to: *"Enforce the legal rights of the citizens of the United States to vote in the several states of this Union* [meaning the Democratic south] *— a right which had been defiantly denied in violation of the Constitution."* In opposition to this bill, **James Bayard, a northern Democrat from Delaware** said: *"This bill is intended not to prevent discrimination between various races of men, but to discriminate directly against the white race in favor of the black race...."*

1871
Democrats Oppose the Force Act of 1871

To strengthen the Enforcement Act of 1870, Republicans introduced the Force Act of 1871 to provide enforcement machinery that would affirmatively insure vindication of the right to vote in all congressional elections. Again the Democrats opposed this legislation. Speaking for the Democrats, Charles Eldredge, a **northern Democrat from Wisconsin**, said: *"Of all the legislation proposed by this or any other Congress, there is none, in my judgment, more unwarrantable and unjustifiable than that proposed by this bill. It is absolutely atrocious. It is hideous and revolting..... It provides a system to drive citizens from the polls and to disgust honest men with our elections. By conferring suffrage upon the colored race, have we lost the rights of our fathers secured to us by the Constitution? In giving freedom to the slaves have we become slaves ourselves?"*

Note: See interview below and Appendix A for reasons why this and other laws were introduced in 1871.

1871
Democrats Attempt to Stop Blacks from Voting

In 1871, several southern blacks were interviewed regarding their voting preferences and the intimidation that they experienced at the polls by the supporters of the Democratic Party. The interviews were documented by the Joint Select Committee to Inquire into Conditions of Affairs in the Late Insurrectionary States. The interviews became a part of *Senate Report No. 579* in the 48th Congress.

On November 1, 1871, John Childers of Livingston, Alabama, was interviewed by the Select Committee. The following is a portion of his interview as documented by Herbert Aptheker in his book, *Documentary History of The Negro People In the United States Vol. 2* (1990, 579):

Question: *Did you ever hear any threats made by **Democrats** against Negroes of what would be done* [to him] *if he voted the radical* [meaning Republican] *ticket?*

Answer: *I have had threats on myself. I can tell them.*

Question: *What kind of threats were made to you?*

Answer: *I have had threats that if we all would vote the **Democratic ticket** we would be well thought of, and the white men of the county – the old citizens of the county – would protect us; and every struggle or trouble we got into we could apply to them for protection, and they would assist us.*

Question: *Where did you hear that said?*

Answer: *I have heard it often. At the last election it was given to me. There was a man standing here in the court-house door; when I started to the ballot-box he told me he had a coffin already made for me, because he thought I was going to vote the radical* [meaning Republican] *ticket.*

Question: *Who was that man?*

Answer: *Well, I am afraid to tell his name, sir.*

Question: *Were the colored folks generally alarmed by these threats, and afraid to vote their true sentiments?*

Answer: *Yes sir, they were.*

Question: *I have heard that a great many colored people voted the **Democratic ticket** at the last governor's election.* [Is that true?]

Answer: *Yes sir.*

Question: *What made them do it?*

Answer: *For fear. I voted myself, I voted the **Democratic ticket**.*

Question: *Were you afraid if you voted the radical ticket you would be harmed?*

Answer: *I was sir; because as I just stated to you, there was a man that told me he had a coffin already made for me. Yes, sir, I voted it, and don't pretend to deny it before nobody. When I was going to the polls there was a man standing in the door and says, "Here comes you, God damn your soul, I have a coffin already made for you." I had two tickets in my pocket then; a **Democratic ticket** and a radial ticket; I pulled out the **Democratic ticket** and showed it to him, and he says, "You are all right, go on."*

1871
Blacks from Kentucky Complain about Democrats

On March 25, 1871, a group of blacks from Kentucky sent a letter to Congress complaining about terrorist attacks initiated by the members of the Democratic Party. The following is a portion of that letter:

To the Senate and House of Representatives in Congress assembled. We the Colored Citizens of Frankfort and vicinity do this day memorialize your honorable bodies upon the condition of affairs now existing in this the state of Kentucky.

We believe you are not familiar with the description of the Ku Klux Klans riding nightly over the country going from county to county and in the county towns spreading terror wherever they go, by robbing, whipping, ravishing, and killing our people without provocation, compelling Colored people to break ice and bathe in the chilly waters of the Kentucky River.

*The Legislature has adjourned - they refused to enact any laws to suppress Ku Klux disorder. We regard them as now being licensed to continue their dark and bloody deeds under the cover of the dark night. They refuse to allow us to testify in the state courts where a white man is concerned. We find their deeds are perpetrated only upon Colored men and white Republicans. We also find that for our services to the Government and our race we have become the special object of hatred and persecution **at the hand of the Democratic Party**. Our people are driven from their homes in great numbers having no redress only in the U.S. Courts which is in many cases unable to reach them. We would state that we have been law abiding citizens, pay our taxes and in many parts of the state our people have been driven from the polls, and refused the right to vote. Many have been slaughtered while attempting to vote, we ask how long is this state of things to last. We appeal to you as law-abiding citizens to enact some laws that will protect us. We see that the* [Democratic] *senators from this state deny there being organized Bands of desperadoes in this state…. The* **Democratic** *Party has here a political organization composed only of* **Democrats** *- not a single Republican can join them. Where many of theses acts have been committed it has been proven that they were the men…. We pray that you will take some steps to remedy these evils.* Signed by:

> *Henry Marrs, Teacher Colored School*
> *Henry Lynn, Livery stable keeper*
> *N.N. Trubro, Grocer*
> *Samuel Damsey, B. Smith,* [Blacksmith]
> *B.T. Crampton, Barber*

See a list of incidents committed by the members of the Democratic Party in the state of Kentucky in Appendix A (Aptheker 1990, 594-599).

1871
The Democrats and Their Klan Connection

In 1871, in response to claims reported by the black citizens of Kentucky and blacks from other states, Republicans sponsored and introduced the Ku Klux Klan Act of 1871. Their goal was to stop the Klan's terrorist activities against blacks and white Republicans primarily in the south. The law was designed to: *(1) Provide civil and criminal sanctions to deter infringements upon civil rights; and (2) to provide authority to the government to meet with force unlawful combinations and violence which interfered with civil rights or the execution of justice or federal law.* One of the spokespersons for the Democratic Party was George Morgan, a **northern Democratic congressman** from Ohio. After hearing of several offenses committed by the Klan, Morgan argued, *"I maintain that if such offenses are committed they have been caused in good part by the mistaken legislation of Congress.... Now sir, if you want to preserve peace in the South, if you want to preserve peace and tranquility in the whole country, if you are not determined to strike a blow which may end the total subversion of our free institutions, change your policy to the South."*

Senator William Stoughton, the Republican from Michigan, countered by presenting both witnesses and the findings of Senate investigations. Stoughton said:

"The evidence taken before the Senate committee in relations to the outrages, lawlessness and violence in North Carolina establishes the following propositions:

1. *The Ku Klux Klan organization exists throughout the State, has a political purpose, and is composed of the **members of the** <u>Democratic</u> Party.*

2. *This organization has sought to carry out its purposes by murders, whippings, intimidation, and violence against its opponents.*

3. *It not only binds its members to execute decrees of crime, but protects them against conviction and punishment, first by disguises and secrecy, and second, by perjury, if necessary, upon the witness-stand and in the jury box.*

4. *Of all the offenders in this order, which has established a reign of terrorism and bloodshed throughout the State, not one has yet been convicted.*

*We may concede, Mr. Speaker, that if this system of violence is to continue in the South, the **Democratic Party** will secure the ascendancy. If political opponents can be marked for slaughter by secret bands of cowardly assassins who ride forth with impunity to execute the decrees upon the unarmed and defenseless, it will be fatal alike to the Republican Party and civil liberty. But sir, we may well ask where will this end? **How long will it be before the Tammany Hall Democrats,** who are now furnishing arms to the Ku Klux Klan of the South to murder southern Republicans, **will introduce this new element of Democratic success into the northern politics?**"*

During an interview with a Klan member, James E. Boyd, Boyd told the Senate Investigative Committee that he was *"initiated into the Ku Klux Klan as an **auxiliary of the Democratic Party**."*

The senator went on to say:

"I have quoted largely from the testimony of this witness for the purpose of showing the dangerous character of this organization. I also make an extract from the testimony of The Honorable Thomas Settle, one of the judges of the Supreme Court, showing the same state of things and strongly corroborating the material statements of Mr. Boyd:

[Chairman interviews first witness]

Question: *Give us your belief as to the true position of the political organizations with reference to this organization [Ku Klux Klan].*

Answer: *Well, sir, I must think that the present* **Democratic Party** *there, judging from the circumstances, are encouraging it. I do not think it is accidental. In the course of our investigation last summer it leaked out in the testimony that Hamilton C. Jones, present member of the Legislature, gave the signs of the Invisible Empire to James E. Boyd, who then a* **Democratic** *candidate for the House of Commons for Alamance county. Dr, Moore, also who had been a member of the previous house, gave the signs of the Invisible Empire....*

The Senator introduces another Klansman.

"The Testimony of Thomas W. Willeford, formerly a member of the Ku Klux Klan, throws additional light upon the secret working of this order and discloses the means by which these results are brought about in the State and local courts. This witness provides the following testimony:

Question: *Did they tell you what the object was?*

Answer: *Yes, sir; in the first meeting. I was initiated in Kennedy's barn.*

Question: *Did you take the oath?*

Answer: *Yes, sir, and then the next Saturday went to the meeting.*

Question: *What did they tell you then was the object of the organization?*

Answer: *They told me it was to damage the Republican Party as much as they could, burning, stealing, whipping* **niggers** *and such things as that.*

Question: *Murder?*

Answer: *The leading men—it was to murder.*

Question: *Have you ever heard of a Ku Klux being convicted of any offense there?*

Answer: *No, sir.*

Question: *Was there anything in the obligation you took or the rules of the order as to your being obliged to defend men by your oath, or otherwise?*

Answer: *Yes, sir: if he could get you in as a witness you had to swear him out, lest you be swearing a lie or not. If you swore against him, why you might just as well be a-traveling at once.*

Question: *You mean by that you would be in danger of your life from the order?*

Answer: *Yes, sir.*

Question: *Anything about getting on the jury?*

Answer: *Yes, sir, if we could get on the jury we could save him, do what you please.*

Question: *No matter what the proof?*

Answer: *Yes, sir, you could not bring proof enough to convict.*

During an interview with a Negro who was a victim of the Klan, the victim told the Senate Investigative Committee how he was shot and left for dead. The following are portions of that interview:

"...The one [Klan member] said, "open the door." I said, "I shouldn't do it." Then one said, "blow his brains out." Just as he said that they all fired through the door.... They shot a half a dozen times or more. I clapped my hand on here [placing his hand on his breast] and said, "they've shot me." My boy knew

where there were some loose planks in the floor. He jerked up two of them and they all run through under the house—all the biggest of them, but the three little girls I had.

Question: *What occurred afterwards?*

Answer: *The next morning I sent for the doctor to come and take out the balls* [gun shots]. *Dr. Montgomery came and took out the balls and told them they had better move me to Graham…or else they won't move me at all. That evening they carried me to Graham and got me there at night.*

Question: *How many balls did they fire into you?*

Answer: *There were five balls.* (The witness indicated where he had been shot – in both arms and in his chest.)

Question: *What has been the effect of such proceedings upon the colored people of that county? Do they feel safe?*

Answer: *They don't feel safe there at all. I can tell you that a great many of them have taken the notion to leave…. They wanted to run them all off <u>because the principal part of them voted the Radical</u>* [Republican] <u>*ticket.*</u>

Question: *Wanted to run all of them off who voted the Radical ticket?*

Answer: *Yes, sir.*

Question: *Did you hear that said?*

Answer: *Yes, sir, I heard it talked and I saw them try it. <u>They tried to turn me from voting the Republican ticket</u>, but I didn't turn and that is why they shot me…. That is the case every election that has been there. They have been trying to get us to vote the* [Democratic] *ticket….*

Question: *Were those that would not vote the* [Democratic] *ticket the ones that had these outrages committed against them?*

Answer: *Yes, sir. You never saw one bothered at all that voted the* [Democratic] *ticket.*

After sharing these interviews with the Senate, Senator Stoughton went on to say:

*The report, Mr. Speaker, to which I have referred shows over one hundred and fifty authenticated cases where persons have either been murdered, brutally beaten, or driven away at the peril of their lives. The **Democratic Party** first denied their association* [with the Ku Klux Klan], *then excused the outrages. In Tennessee, and other southern states, the laws passed by Republican Legislatures to suppress and punish the **Ku Klux Klan** were repealed as soon as the **Democratic Party** came back into power. The relation of the **Democratic Party** to the **Klan** is precisely that of the receiver of stolen property to the thief. The murder of leading Republicans, terrifying the colored population and putting whole neighborhoods in fear so that the **Klan** can control an election, is heralded as a **Democratic** victory.*

Nation's Top Historians Show Klan and Democratic Connection

History scholars report that when Republicans passed various pieces of legislation and developed a number of social programs to assist blacks (i.e., Freedmen Bureau), Democrats became very angry and resentful as expressed in many of their political platforms. From their deep-seated anger, several terrorist organizations were *born*—and in their efforts to gain the upper hand the Democrats became the "*daddy*" of the Ku Klux Klan. The scholars of the *Encyclopedia Britannica* reported that the "***Democrat's*** *resentment led to the formation of the secret terroristic organizations such as the Ku Klux Klan and the Knights of the White Camelia. The use of fraud,*

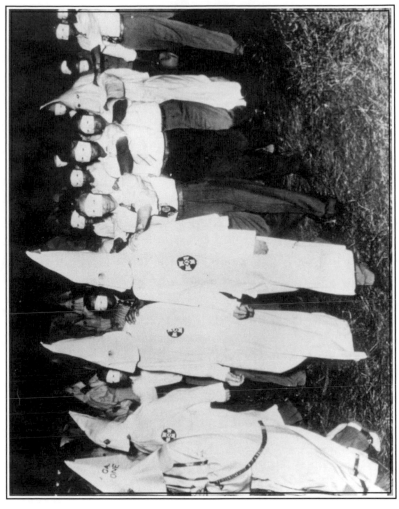

Senate investigations and our nation's top historians reveal the connection between the Klan and the Democratic Party. The Democratic Party was also known as the Party of White Supremacy.

violence and intimidation helped Southern conservatives regain control of their state governments...." (1992, 979)

In *Reconstruction: The Great Experiment*, Professor Allen Trelease said:

"*Klansmen in disguise rode through Negro neighborhoods at night warning Negroes either to cast **Democratic** ballots or stay away from the polls. The Klan also sent notices to Republican office holders, warning them of death and telling them to either resign or leave the vicinity. Similar notices went to active **Republicans of both races** and often to the teachers of **Negro schools as well**. Klan activities created a reign of terror in many localities and sometimes had the desired effect of demoralizing Negroes and Republicans.... **Republicans** of both races were threatened, beaten, shot, and murdered with impunity. In some areas Negroes stopped voting or voted **the Democrat** ticket as the Klan demanded....**Democrats**, by a kind of tortured reasoning, sometimes accused Negroes and Republicans of attacking and even killing each other so that the crimes would be blamed on the **Democrats**.*

Professors John Hope Franklin and Alfred Moss, authors of *From Slavery to Freedom* tell us that:

"*The Camelias and the Klan were the most powerful of the secret orders. Armed with guns, swords, or other weapons, their members patrolled some parts of the South day and night. They used intimidation, force, ostracism in business and society, bribery at the polls, arson, and even murder to accomplish their deed. Depriving the Negro of political equality became, to them, a holy crusade in which a noble end justified any means. Negroes were run out of communities if they disobeyed orders to desist from voting, and the more resolute and therefore insubordinate blacks were whipped, maimed, and hanged. In 1871 several Negro officials in South*

*Carolina were given fifteen days to resign and they were warned that if they failed to do so, then retributive justice will as surely be used as night follows day. For many white Southerners violence was still the surest means of keeping the Negroes politically impotent, and in countless communities they were not allowed, under penalties of reprisals, to show their faces in town on Election Day. It had looked as though the Civil War would break out anew as the **Democrats resorted to every possible device to overthrow the radicals**.*

In *Reconstruction after the Civil War*, Professor Franklin and Alfred Moss said:

*It was reported that in North Carolina the Klan was responsible for 260 outrages, including 7 murders and the whipping of 72 whites and 141 Negroes. In one county in South Carolina 6 men were murdered and more than 300 were whipped during the first six months of 1870. The personal indignities inflicted upon individual white **and Negroes were so varied and so numerous as to defy classification or enumeration** (157).*

In his book, *The Abolitionist Legacy*, Professor James McPherson reported, *"In 1873, Louisiana became almost a synonym for chaos and violence. When Grant sent federal troops to install Kellogg in office* [as governor], **Louisiana Democrats** *were infuriated. They formed White Leagues which attacked black and white Republicans and took scores of lives.*(40)

From his book entitled *Charles Sumner*, Harvard Professor David Hebert Donald reached the following conclusion: *Congress could give the Negro the vote, but all over the South the **Ku Klux Klan and other terrorist organizations systematically intimidated the freedmen,** flogged or slaughtered their leaders and drove whites who worked with them into exile. Congress could require federal troops* *to supervise the registration of voters, but Negroes were waylaid and butchered on the roads to the registration offices. Congress could suppress outright violence by military force, but it could do nothing to protect Negroes from landlords who told them bluntly: If you vote with that Yankee [Republican] party you shall not live on our land* (420).

Professor Howard O. Linsay, the author of *A History of Black Americans* says, *"Blacks and sympathetic Whites were attacked and threatened. African Americans were discouraged from seeking elected office and even from trying to vote. Any and all means were used, from threats, to violence, to outright murder"* (88-89). (Note: For specific attacks, see Appendices A and B.)

1873
14th Amendment Weakened by Supreme Court

On April 14, 1873, the United States Supreme Court issued its ruling on the challenge of the meaning of the *Privileges or Immunities Clause* of the 14th Amendment. The case was called the *Slaughterhouse Cases*. Although the case did not directly have anything to do with blacks, it had an indirect impact on subsequent civil rights litigation. Legal experts say the narrow interpretation of the 14th Amendment in this case made a *clear distinction between the rights of the state and national citizenship that had not been in the minds of framers*, thus it took away or limited the national government's power to intervene in matters at the state level, because the rights of national citizenship versus state citizenship were now legally defined. The decision opened the door to a multitude of racist practices at the state level, while limiting federal intervention. The final ruling in the case of *Plessy v. Ferguson* and other subsequent civil rights cases was affected and influenced by the *Slaughterhouse* decision (Companion 2005, 924).

1874
Blacks from Alabama Write Congress about Democrats

In 1874, blacks from Alabama sent Congress the following letter.

(Portions of) Petition to the President of the United States and to U.S. Congress

From Blacks of Alabama in 1874

...As a race, and as citizens, we never have enjoyed, except partially, imperfectly, and locally, our political and civil rights in this State. Our right to vote in elections has been, in a large portion of this state, denied, abridged, and rendered difficult and dangerous ever since we became voters. The means used by our political opponents [Democrats] *to destroy or impair our right have been various; but chiefly consisted of violence in the form of secret assassinations, lynching, intimidation, malicious and frivolous prosecutions and arrest. And by depriving or threatening to deprive us of employment and renting of lands, which many of us, in our poverty and distress, were unable to disregard. These acts of lawlessness have been repeated and continued since our first vote in 1868, and their effect has been such that from 10,000 to 15,000 of the votes of our race have in each election been either repressed or been given under compulsion to our political opponents.*

A secret, powerful, vindictive, and dangerous organization composed exclusively of white men belonging to the **Democratic Party** *in this state, and whose objects were to control the labor and repress or control the votes of the Colored citizens of this state. That organization, or a substitute and successor to it, under a changed name and a somewhat changed wardrobe and personal manifestation, still exist in all its hideous and fearful proportions. This organization we* *solemnly believe pervades all of the late rebellious States, and contains more than 100,000 arm-bearing men, most of who are experienced and skilled in war. The definite <u>political object of this organization</u> is, by terror and violence, to make the citizenship and franchise of the Colored race, as established by the Constitution of the United States practically and substantially a nullity* (Aptheker 1990, 600-604).

Professor John Hope Franklin said, *"With the new franchise laws, with careful administration by white registrars who knew what they were doing and with effective exclusion of Blacks from <u>Democratic</u> primaries, white supremacy in the realm of politics seemed to be permanently established."*

1875
Southern Democrats Introduce Jim Crow

Southern Democrats from the state of Tennessee legislated our nation's first Jim Crow laws. The laws mandated that blacks be confined to separate sections of trains, depots, and wharves. Southern states under Democratic control expanded the use of such laws to include many other facilities as well, including separate restrooms, drinking fountains, public parks, and cemeteries. Eventually, blacks were banned from white barbershops, hotels, restaurants, theaters, and in some states they were required to swear on separate Bibles in courtroom proceedings. The Jim Crow laws along with the new Black Codes (both initiated by Southern Democrats) had a devastating impact on the newly freed slaves. Some historians believed these laws and codes created conditions far worse than slavery. The Jim Crow laws were merely laws specifically designed by southern Democrats to keep African Americans in their place. The national party never condemned these laws. Seven years earlier (1868), it was the national Democratic Party that said: *"This is a white man's country, let the white man rule."*

1875
Republicans Introduce New Civil Rights Law

In 1875, Republicans sponsored and introduced the Civil Rights Act of 1875. The purpose of this law was *"to obtain equality in Public Accommodations."* The law stated the following:

Be it enacted by the Senate and House of Representatives of the United States of America in Congress assembled. That all persons within the jurisdiction of the United States shall be entitled to the full and equal enjoyment of the accommodations, advantages, facilities and privileges of inns, public conveyances on land or water, theaters, and other places of amusement; subject only to the conditions and limitation established by law, and applicable alike to citizens of every race and color, regardless of any previous condition of servitude....

The bill was introduced by Republican Senator Charles Sumner. He died on March 11, 1874, one year before the bill was passed. **Republican Senator Frederick Frelinghuysen of New Jersey** opened up the debate. The senator said, *"There is but one idea in the bill, and that is: The equality of races before the law. The language of this bill secures full and equal privileges in schools subject to laws which do not discriminate as to color. The bill provides that full and equal privileges shall be enjoyed by all persons in public schools supported by taxation, subject only to the limitation established by law, applicable alike to citizens of every race and color and regardless of previous servitude. **The object of the bill is to destroy, not recognize the distinctions of race.**"*

One of the spokespersons for the Democrats was **Willard Saulsbury, a northern Democrat from Delaware**. In response to Frelinghuysen's statement, Saulsbury said:

There is coming a day when the American people will hold you and your [Republican] *party to a strict responsibility for present indifference to their wishes and for the great wrong you propose by this bill to inflict upon them. What is this measure? Disguise it as you may, it is nothing more nor less than an attempt on the part of the American Congress to enforce association and companionship between the races in this country. The object of this bill is not to confer upon the colored race any political rights. It proposes to enforce familiarity, association, and companionship between the white and colored people of this country. Is not that true? That is the object of this bill. It proposes so far as hotels are concerned that the white and the colored people shall have the save advantages, equal advantages; that they shall enter with equal right into every part of the inn; that the keeper of the inn shall make no discrimination on account of their race or color; that colored men shall sit at the same table beside the white guest, that he shall enter the same parlor and take his seat beside the wife and daughter of the white man, whether the white man is willing or not, because you prohibit discrimination against him. If the object was not to enforce companionship, why do you not permit in this bill the landlord to set apart a portion of the parlor for white people, so that he might have one table for the colored man and another table for the white man, giving to one as good accommodations as the other? Why is it that there is not a provision which allows that? Simply because, I say, the object and purpose of this bill is force association and companionship between the races.* The debates took place April 29-May 22, 1874.

Note: In 1964, during their arguments *against* the passage of the 1964 Civil Rights Act, Democrats claimed that the 1964 Civil Rights Act was merely the reactivation of the Republican's previous 1875 Civil Rights Act that they (the Democrats) had declared "unconstitutional" by the United States Supreme Court. See debates on 1964 Civil Rights Act.

1877
Republicans Make a Deal with Democrats

In 1877, Republicans reached an ill-advised compromise with the Democrats. The compromise gave the Republicans the White House but required that the national government remove all federal troops from the south. Although the Democrats had their way with blacks while the troops were present, Democrats felt the removal of the troops would give them more flexibility to rule the South without the possible interference of the federal government.

1883
Democrats Have 1875 Civil Right Act
Declared Unconstitutional

Known as the *Civil Rights Cases of 1881*, the court ruled in an 8-to-1 decision on October 15, 1883, that the Republicans' 1875 Civil Rights Act was unconstitutional. The court held that the 1875 Civil Rights Act was an *impermissible attempt* by the Republican Congress *to create a municipal code regulating the private conduct of individuals in the area of racial discrimination and that even private interference with such rights as voting, jury service, or appearing as witnesses in state court were not within the province of Congress to control* (Hall 2005, 173). The *Slaughterhouse decision* had a direct impact on the outcome of this case.

1884
Older Blacks Knew Democrats Were Racist

On February 18, 1884, Mrs. Violet Keeling was interviewed by the Senate Select Committee on voting irregularities in the Democrat-controlled south. The following is a portion of that interview:

Question: *Are any of the colored people in your county* **Democrats***?*

Answer: *I don't know. I don't have nothing to do with that sort.*

Question*: I ask you if any of them are* **Democrats***.*

Answer: *I am telling you just what I know; I don't have nothing to do with that sort.*

Question: *Why do you have such a dislike to a colored man that votes the* **Democratic ticket***?*

Answer: *I will tell you as near as I know. I think that if the race of colored people that has got no friends no how, and if they don't hang together they won't have none while one party is going one way and another the other. I don't wish to see a colored man sell himself when he can do without. Of course we all have to live, and I always like to have a man live even if he works for 25 cents a day, but I don't want to see him sell himself away.*

Question: *Cannot a colored man vote the* **Democratic ticket** *without selling himself?*

Answer*: I think if a colored man votes the* **Democratic ticket** *he has already sold himself, because the white man is no friend to him anyway.*

Question*: Suppose your husband should go and vote a* **Democratic ticket***?*

Answer*: I would just pick up my clothes and go to my father's, if I had a father, or would go to work for 25 cents a day* (Aptheker 1990, 739-740).

1888
Blacks from New Orleans Write Congress

In 1888, several black ministers from New Orleans came together and wrote a letter to Congress. The following is a portion of that letter:

<u>To the People of the United States:</u>

We, the citizens of New Orleans, as well as of neighboring parishes, from which we have been driven away without warrant or law, assembled in mass meeting at New Orleans, Louisiana, on Wednesday, August 22, 1888, at Geddes Hall, declare and assert: That a reign of terror exists in many parts of the state; that the laws are suspended and the officers of the government, <u>from the governor down</u>, afford no protection to the lives and property of the people against armed bodies of whites, who shed innocent blood and commit deeds of savagery unsurpassed in the dark ages of mankind.

*For the past twelve years we have been most effectively disfranchised and robbed of our political rights. While denied the privilege in many places of voting for the party and candidates of our choice, acts of violence have been committed to compel us to vote against the dictates of our conscience for the **Democratic Party**, and the Republican ballots cast by us have been counted for the **Democratic candidates**. The press, the pulpit, the commercial organizations, and executive authority of the State have given both open and silent approval of all these crimes. In addition to these methods, there seems to be a deep scheme to reduce the Negroes of the State to a condition of abject serfdom and peonage.*

These acts are done in deliberate <u>defiance of the Constitution and the laws of the United States</u>, which are so thoroughly nullified that the Negroes who bore arms in defense of the Union have no protection or shelter from them within the *borders of Louisiana. During the past twelve months our people have suffered from the lawless regulators as never before and since the carnival of bloodshed conducted by the* <u>*Democratic Party*</u> *in 1868.*

A single volume would scarcely afford sufficient space to enumerate the outrage our people have suffered, and are daily suffering at the hand of their oppressors. They are flagrantly deprived of every right guaranteed them by the Constitution; in many parts of the State they are free only in name; they cannot assemble in places to indicate and discuss an equitable rate of wages for their labor; they do not feel safe as property holders and tax-payers, and are permitted to enjoy but very few public conveniences.

To our people we advise calmness and a strict regard for law and order. If your homes are invaded expect no mercy, for none will be shown, and if doomed to die, then die defending your life and home to the best of your ability. If convinced that you will not be permitted to live where you are in peace and perfect security, quietly go away.

"Invoking the guiding favor of Almighty God and the sympathy of mankind, we are your brethren in affliction and the common bond of humanity (Aptheker 1990, 741-743).

The letter was signed by, Rev. Ernest Lyon, Rev. A.E.P. Albert, Rev. J.H. Coker, M.D., Rev. T.B. Stamps, Rev. M.C.B. Mason, Rev. W. Paul Green, Rev. J. D. Kennedy and Rev. C.B. Wilson. The problems were so severe during the Grant administration that he had to send troops to the South to protect Black voters from the Democrats and their Klan supporters.

1892
Democrats Platform Oppose Federal Marshals

In the Democrats' 1892 Platform they stated that they were opposed to *"Federal Marshals at every polling place"* to monitor voting irregularities (as they pertain to black voters) in states controlled by Democrats.

1894
Democrats Appeal Civil Rights Legislation

Law Professor, Bernard Schwartz of the New York University School of Law said: *"The post-Civil War amendments and statutes in the field of civil rights, from the Thirteenth Amendment, December 18, 1863 to the Civil Rights Act of 1875, had been strongly opposed by the **Democratic Party**. Hence, it was natural that when the party first won back the Presidency and control of both houses of Congress in 1892, its leaders should seek to undo much of the Republican civil rights program (Statutory History of the United States Civil Rights 1970, 803).*

In 1892, Democrats introduced the Repeal Act of 1894 to repeal all statutes relating to: *"supervisors of elections and deputy marshals, as well as federal protection of the right to vote."* Republican opposition: Leading the debate against the bill were Republican Congressman Marriott Brosius of Pennsylvania, and Republican Senator George Hoar of Massachusetts.

On October 10, 1893, the bill passed in the House with 201 voting for it and 102 against it. On February 7, 1894, it passed in the Senate. Thirty-nine voted for it and 28 voted against it. Just before the final vote, Republican Senator Hoar of Massachusetts presented the following argument:

*Wherever there is a crevice in our protection of the freedom of the ballot there you will find the **Democratic Party** trying* *to break through. Wherever we have left open an opportunity to get possession of an office contrary to the true and constitutional will of the majority there you will find that party pressing; there you will find that party exercising an ingenuity before which even the great inventive genius of American People exerted in other directions fails and is insignificant in the comparison.*

*In one State, Mississippi, in order to **disfranchise** [black] **Republicans who cannot read and write** and let [white] **Democrats** who can not read and write vote, there is a constitutional provision by which **Democratic** election officers determine whether the understanding of the voters who can not read or write has a fit and sufficient understanding of the Constitution; and, although that was denounced by able **Democrats** holding high public positions both in Washington and Mississippi, the proposition finds defenders on this floor, Senators gravely comparing it to the provision of the constitution of Massachusetts....*

*In Delaware, it is necessary that a tax should be paid a certain time beforehand, and, accordingly, unless they are much belied, the **Democratic** tax collector runs away when the Republican comes to pay their taxes....*

*Mr. President, this is a question of fraud or no fraud. They tell us that there have been some Republican invasions of the elective franchise, and it is quite possible, but where can you find one well-authenticated case of a man who has been deprived or inconvenienced in the exercise of his franchise by these United States marshals or other officers, I will pledge myself to find ten thousand well established by evidence on record here where without those securities Republicans have been deprived of their votes by **Democratic** practices. I incur no danger in making that challenge. If you will produce me a citizen of the United States, a **Democrat,** who lost his honest* *vote in consequence of intimidation or impediment, created by these United States marshals, I will find on record here the proof of ten thousand Republicans who have lost their votes by **Democratic** practices....*

Mr. President, the nation must protect its own. Every citizen whose right is imperiled if he be but one, when it is a right of national citizenship and a right conferred and enjoyed under the Constitution of the United States, has the right to demand for its protection the entire force of the United States until the Army has spent its last man and the Navy fired its last gun. Most of us have nothing else than the right to vote.... The urn in which the American cast his ballot ought to be, aye, and it shall be, as sacred as a sacramental vessel.

1896
Democrats Take Segregation Issues to Court and Win

In 1896, Democrats won another major landmark decision in the case of *Plessy v. Ferguson*. The case legalized and endorsed the Democrats' Jim Crow segregation policies. This *"separate but equal"* ruling had a profound effect on the **entire black race** in both the north and the south.

In his book: *The Statutory History of the United States – Civil Rights*, Professor Bernard Schwartz writes: "*In* Plessy v. Ferguson *the Supreme Court construed the equal protection clause in a manner which enabled discrimination against the Negro to be condoned by law...* Plessy v. Ferguson *gave the lie to the American ideal, so eloquently stated by Justice John Harlan in dissent there: 'Our Constitution is color blind, and neither knows or tolerates classes among citizens.' Upon Plessy was built the whole structure of segregation that has been at the heart of the [Democrats'] southern system of racial discrimination. So much was, indeed conceded by the Supreme Court itself, including the 1873 Slaughter House Cases, 16 Wall. 36 (1873)...."* (360)

1898
Democrats Launch a Racist Political Campaign

In 1898, the **Democrats** carried out their racist political agenda in Wilmington, North Carolina, when they successfully drove black Republicans out of office by rigging the 1898 election and killing several blacks in the process. The Democrats' campaign theme was: *"saving our white women"* [from the middle class blacks who controlled Wilmington at the time] and their official campaign slogan was one word: *"Nigger."* Shortly after the Wilmington massacre, riots broke out in other parts of the south, and 101 blacks were lynched. In 2007, the Executive Committee of the Democratic Party of North Carolina (consisting of seven hundred party leaders from one hundred counties) issued the following apology to the African American community of North Carolina.

❖ WHEREAS, One of the most indelible events in North Carolina and American history occurred on November 17, 1898, when the city of Wilmington erupted in a bloody riot in which dozens of African Americans—including businessmen, community leaders, journalists, and elected officials—were murdered and banished from the city along with many of their white allies; and

❖ WHEREAS, Public knowledge and historical memory of this event was obscure until the North Carolina General Assembly, led by Representative Thomas E. Wright and the late Senator Luther Jordan, both Democrats, established the Wilmington Race Riot Commission in 2000 to develop a historical record of the event and to assess the economic impact of the riot on African Americans in Wilmington and across the Eastern region and state; and

❖ WHEREAS, The Commission, chaired by Representative Wright and Democratic Senator Julia Boseman, both of Wilmington, oversaw a formal investigation of the events of 1898 and approved a 464-page report, detailing the history of the riot and the events that precipitated it; and

❖ WHEREAS, The Commission's report concluded that past leaders of the North Carolina Democratic Party were directly responsible for and participants in the violence of November 17, 1898; and

❖ WHEREAS, The report also concluded that the North Carolina Democratic Party engineered and executed a state-wide white supremacy campaign in order to win the 1900 elections that was vicious, polarizing, and defamatory toward African Americans and that encouraged racial violence; and

❖ WHEREAS, The effects of that campaign and the Wilmington Riots lasted far beyond 1898, paving the way for legislation that disenfranchised African American and poor white citizens, for lynching and violence against black citizens, and for Jim Crow segregation until the Civil Rights Movement of the 1960s; and

❖ WHEREAS, The North Carolina Democratic Party embraces the Commission's report as a chronicle of an important part of State history, but it is shocked to learn the full extent of past party leaders' involvement in the Wilmington Riot of 1898 as these deplorable actions contradict the spirit, philosophy, platform, and policies of today's North Carolina Democratic Party; now, therefore, be it

❖ RESOLVED, That the North Carolina Democratic Party both acknowledges and renounces the actions of past Party leaders involved in the events of 1898 and those actions' impact on the State of North Carolina and the United States of America; and

❖ RESOLVED, That the North Carolina Democratic Party apologizes to those who were affected by the actions - and their repercussions—of past party leaders....

1899
Blacks Complain about Democratic South

In 1899, the *New York Tribune* published the concerns of the National Afro-American Council of the United States (on May 4, 1899). Herbert Aptheker records the following in his: *Documentary History of the Negro People in the United States*. The council stated:

The National Afro-American Council of the United States has issued a proclamation calling upon the colored people of this country to set apart Friday, June 2nd, as a day of fasting and prayer, and has called upon all colored ministers to devote the sunrise hour of the following Sunday, June 4th, to special exercises in order that God, the Father of Mercies, may take our deplorable case in His own hands, and that if vengeance is to be meted out, let God Himself repay.

We are dragged before the courts by the thousands and sentenced to every form of punishment, and even executed, without the privilege of having a jury composed in whole or part of members of our own race, while simple justice should guarantee us judges and juries who could adjudicate our case free from the bias, caste and prejudice incident to the same in this country.

In many sections [of the Democratic South] we are arrested and lodged in jails on the most frivolous suspicion of being perpetrators of the most hideous and revolting crimes, and, regardless of established guilt, mobs are formed of ignorant, vicious, whiskey besotted men, at whose approach the keys of these jails and prisons are surrendered and the suspicioned party is ruthlessly forced from the custody of the law and tortured, hanged, shot, butchered, dismembered and burned in the most fiendish manner. These mobs no longer conceal themselves in the shadows of the night, but in open day plunder the prisons for the victims of their lawless vengeance and defiantly walk into courts and rob the sheriffs and judges of their prisoners and butcher them without even time to commune in prayer with God, a privilege that no barbaric age has ever denied a soul about to be ushered into the presence of his Maker. (799-803)

1900
Democratic States Still Racist

By the turn of the century, in areas controlled by **Democrats** (the South), thousands of blacks were placed in hardcore prison labor camps. According to historians, the prison camps were *worse than slavery*—and represented a new source of free forced labor. The prisoners were required to work from ten to fourteen hours a day, six to seven days a week in temperatures above 100 degrees and below 0. <u>One-fourth of the prison population were black children ages six to eighteen.</u> Twelve-year old Cy Williams, was sentenced to twenty years of hard labor for allegedly stealing a horse that he was too small to ride. Eight-year old Will Evans was sentenced to two years of hard labor for taking some change from a counter, and six-year old Mary Gay was sentenced to thirty days of hard labor for taking a hat. While southern authorities sent whites to *jail* for the same offenses (with shorter sentences), they sent blacks to the *prison labor camps* with longer sentences. The camps provided free labor for building railroads, for draining snake and alligator infested swamps and rivers, and for mining coal. Conditions in these camps were harsh—blacks were transported from one project to another in rolling cages, similar to those used for circus animals. While thousands died from malaria, frostbite, heat strokes, and shackle poisoning, others were buried alive in mines, blown to pieces during mine explosions, and many others were drowned or shot and beaten to death. <u>Every southern black was a potential prisoner</u>, which meant that the southern owners of railroads and mines had an unlimited resource of free labor. Historians say the prison labor system was the Democrats' **new form of slavery** – but more inhumane than the institution of slavery.

1904
Democrat Produces Popular Racist Stage Play

In 1904, Thomas Dixon opened his new stage play (*The Klansman*) in Atlanta, Georgia. The play glorified the Klan and defamed blacks by portraying blacks as savaged men on the prowl for white women. During the week of September 17, an Atlanta newspaper falsely reported rapes of a few white women. Their false reports resulted in several thousand white men gathering in the streets of Atlanta, mercilessly beating blacks at random. When blacks fought back, they were killed. The Militia was called in to control the rioting.

1909
NAACP was Formed to Stop Lynchings

As an answer to the lynchings and other racist practices by Democrats, three whites came together and formed a new organization. The organization was called the NAACP, or the National Association for the Advancement of Colored People.

African American History Professor, John Hope Franklin said, *"In 1909, liberal whites such as Mary White Ovington, Oswald Garrison Villard, and William English Walling issued a call for a conference to consider the plight of African Americans.* In that same year, these key individuals met and formed what is now known as the NAACP. In confirming Professor Franklin's findings, the Negro Almanac reports that the formation of the *"NAACP was largely the brain-child of Ovington, Villard and Walling, three white individuals"* (Ploski and Williams 1989, 260). By 1936, these individuals and other white liberals continued to play a major role in the NAACP, focusing primarily on eliminating the lynching of black citizens in states under Democratic control.

1909
Democratic Senator Justifies Lynching

On March 23, 1909, Democratic senator, Ben Tillman of South Carolina told the members of the United States Senate that he defended violence against black men, claiming that: *"southern white women will not submit to the black man gratifying his lust on our wives and daughters without lynching him."* During another speech Tillman told America: *"We reorganized the **Democratic Party** with one plank and only one plank, namely, that this is a white man's country and white men must govern it."*

1912
Woodrow Wilson Turns His Back on Dubois

In 1912, W.E.B Dubois endorsed **Democratic** candidate, Woodrow Wilson for president. He asked Wilson to support *black education, the blacks' rights to vote and own land, and to stop the onslaught of lynchings*. Shortly after Wilson took office, he ignored Dubois' request and gave his blessings to three southern cabinet members to segregate their departments. A New York paper released an article entitled: *"Jim Crow has come to Washington."* One government supervisor boasted that: *"There are no government positions for Negroes in the South, a Negro's place is in the cornfield."*

1915
Racist Democrat Produces Hit Movie

In 1915, the stage play, *The Klansman,* was made into a motion picture. The movie, *The Birth of a Nation*, was produced by D.W. Griffith, a loyal Democrat and the son of a Confederate officer and Kentucky legislator. The film strengthened the Klan, and its membership grew. In many places where **Democrats** were in control, gangs of whites openly attacked blacks on the street after watching the movie.

1917
Blacks Attacked in Democratic State

In 1917, black soldiers in Houston, Texas, who had been harassed for several months by the Houston police, took matters into their own hands after one of their soldiers was arrested and beaten without cause. One hundred black soldiers went to town to retaliate. Shots were fired. Sixteen whites and four fellow black soldiers were killed. Nineteen soldiers were court-martialed and sentenced to death. The soldiers were denied the right to appeal their case to Woodrow Wilson, the same Democratic President whom W.E.B Dubois had previously endorsed.

1918
Black Mother Lynched in Democrats' Georgia

In May of 1918, there was a series of lynching in the state of Georgia. When Mary Turner, who was nine-months pregnant, complained that she was going to see to it that the white men who lynched her husband would be prosecuted, the mob dragged her from her home, tortured her, and hung her from a tree. While she was hanging from the rope, they cut open her womb, the child spilled out, and when the baby cried, they crushed the baby's skull with the heels of their boots.

1919
Democrats' Racist Acts Reaches Chicago

During the Senate debates on the Ku Klux Klan Act of 1871, Republican Senator William Stoughton asked, *"How long will it be before the Tammany Hall Democrats, who are now furnishing arms to the Ku Klux Klan of the south to murder southern Republicans, will introduce this new element of Democratic success into the northern politics?"* His question was answered on July 27, 1919, when a race riot broke out after whites attacked and killed Eugene Williams, a black swimmer in Chicago. When the dust settled, fifteen whites and twenty-three blacks were killed. *"Jim Crow," said the* Chicago Tribune*, "has come north."*

1919
Black Farmers Massacred in Democratic South

In 1919, in Elaine, Arkansas, historians report that as many as 200 black farmers were massacred and several others were arrested and executed simply because they met at a black church to discuss how they could stop their white landlords from cheating them out of their cotton crops. No one was arrested, tried, or convicted for this massacre.

1921
Black Community Destroyed in Democratic South

On May 31, 1921, Tulsa's leading newspaper, the *Tulsa Tribune*, released a front-page article alleging that a black man had raped a white woman. Whites went on a rampage, killing three hundred blacks, wounding eight hundred others, and arresting as many as six thousand. During the riot, whites burned the entire middle class black community, an area that consisted of thirty-five city blocks. The area was known as the Greenwood District or Black Wall Street. Even though blacks lost all of their businesses and scores of lives, no white was arrested or convicted for this act of terror.

1922
Black Community Burned in Democratic South

On December 31, 1922, a young white woman in Rosewood, Florida, claimed she was raped by a black man. The next day (New Year's Day) several whites from nearby communities swarmed the town killing over one hundred blacks and burning down most of the black-owned businesses and homes. The massacre included women and children. Others escaped by spending the night in nearby swamps. No whites were arrested, tried, or convicted for this brutal massacre. **Democratic** Governor Cary Hardee took no action. Reparations were finally paid in 1993.

The NAACP protested against the multitude of lynchings that took place in states controlled by Democrats.

1933
Democratic President Ignores Black Concerns

In 1933, **Democratic** presidential candidate, Franklin D. Roosevelt won the black vote and became the thirty-second president of the United States. Professor John Hope Franklin says that, shortly after Roosevelt took office, blacks *"discovered that agencies of the federal government were as capable of discriminatory practices, or could be used for such purposes, as any others. Black sharecroppers and tenants had difficulty in obtaining relief benefits from the Agricultural Administration because landlords kept their relief checks. While the Federal Housing Authority guaranteed a limited number of loans for Negroes to build or purchase homes, its policy was not to interfere with local housing practices that excluded Negroes from certain neighborhoods. Lynchings and other forms of racial violence had continued during the New Deal and the federal government had pleaded that it had no jurisdiction over such matters."* President Roosevelt also banned black newspapers from military bases, claiming they were *"communist."* These were the same black newspapers that had urged their readers to give Roosevelt their vote.

In his book, *The Party of the People: A History of the Democrats*, Julies Witcover says, *"Roosevelt demonstrated that while he may have been generally sympathetic to the cause of civil rights for black Americans, he was not going to go out of his way for them when to do so would jeopardize his other objectives.... FDR never clearly defined civil rights goals...."* While Eleanor Roosevelt came out in support of an anti-lynching bill, Roosevelt continued to *"express encouragement to the black leadership to maintain its efforts –without his help"* (175).

1945
Truman Ignores Need for Lynching Laws

In 1945, Vice President Harry S. Truman, became president of the United States. Although he was elected with a civil rights platform, it was under pressure and threats by A. Phillip Randolph that he signed an Executive Order to integrate the military. No civil rights legislation was passed during his administration to stop the ongoing lynchings in the south. Historians report that southern blacks lived in constant fear, knowing that death at the hands of their Democratic terrorists was just a matter of time. See a list of those who were victims of lynchings in **Appendix B**.

1954
Democrats' Major Defeat on Segregation

On May 17, 1954, in an effort to legally maintain policies of segregation, Democrats suffered a major defeat when the United States Supreme Court rendered its decision in the landmark case of ***Brown v. Board of Education***. The decision virtually dismantled the earlier ruling in the case of ***Plessy v. Ferguson***. Southern Democrats were furious and continued their practices of *segregation* in defiance of the ruling. Shortly after the *Brown* decision, over one hundred Democratic congressmen signed the **Southern Manifesto** as commitment to continue the fight to maintain segregated schools. Two Republicans representing a southern state were pressured to also sign the racist document. (See Appendix C for a copy of the document.) No matter what the cost, Democrats were determined to deny blacks a quality education as they had during the previous one hundred years.

Princeton University's history professor, James McPherson reports, that after the Civil War, when the American Missionary Association (AMA) sent white teachers to the Democratic

South to educate Negroes, the old time southern *hospitality* was immediately transformed into southern *hostility.*

Professor McPherson said:

Southern hostility to Yankee teachers sometimes went beyond ostracism and verbal abuse. In times of political excitement during Reconstruction many missionaries were threatened, beaten, and murdered. The AMA reported several incidents similar to the one in which a group of masked men took a teacher from his house in North Carolina in 1874, tied him up, and after threatening to kill him if he did not leave the state gave him 100 lashes with a bullwhip. The founder and president for nearly 30 years of Shaw University, Henry Tupper of Massachusetts, was often harassed by the Ku Klux Klan and once hid all night in a cornfield with his wife and two children to avoid an assassination attempt.

In 1871, a college treasurer went to a nearby town on business, had dinner with a Black family, and after leaving a prayer meeting at a Negro church was ambushed by five men who fired at him seven times and left him for dead. The shots had missed, however, the treasurer returned to his hotel, where at 3:00 AM 30 masked men dragged him from his bed, took him to the woods, and gave him 61 lashes with a hickory whip.

The 1874 elections were a particularly tense time; as one teacher put it, to be for weeks in a constant expectation of being murdered or burned out, and without losing faith in God, is something of a strain on the nerves.

In 1879, the Northern Methodists compiled a list of 34 attacks on their missionaries and teachers in the past decade; 19 of the victims were White and 15 Black, three of the whites and four of the Blacks were killed.

The AMA tried for several years to cooperate with local [southern] *school boards. So long as <u>Republicans</u> were in* *power this arrangement worked out reasonably well. But when the Democrats began to regain control of the South the dual support foundered and eventually collapsed. In Memphis, the Democrats dismissed all AMA teachers, forcing the association to withdraw from the jointly sponsored Lincoln School and found LeMoyne Institute in its place. In Columbus, Mississippi, Democrats drove out the Union Academy's northern teachers with threats of violence and then closed the school in 1871"* (McPherson 1975, 174-175).

1955
Chicago Black Teenager Killed in Democratic South

In 1955, while visiting relatives in Mississippi, a fourteen-year-old black teenager from Chicago named Emmett Till was abducted, severely beaten, and thrown into a river with a weight fastened around his neck with barbed wire. The fear of retaliation from local Democratic officials kept many witnesses from testifying. Two white men who were arrested for the murder were eventually acquitted. In 2004, President G.W. Bush asked his Justice Department to re-open the Emmett Till case.

1955
Montgomery Bus Boycott

On December 5, 1955, the black community of Montgomery, Alabama, launched a bus boycott to protest against discriminatory practices in the city's transportation system. Local Democratic officials opposed the boycott and did everything to discourage it.

1957
Democratic Governor Uses National Guard

In 1957, fifteen-year old Elizabeth Eckford was one of nine black students chosen by school authorities in Little Rock, Arkansas, to desegregate a local high school. The state's Democratic governor ordered the National Guard to turn the black students away. As black students throughout the Democratic-controlled south attempted to register for school, crowds of white students chanted, *"Two, four, six, eight, we don't want to integrate."*

1957
Democrats' Opposition to 1957 Civil Rights Act

Introduced by Republican President, Dwight D. Eisenhower in 1957 and supported by a *bipartisan* Congress, the 1957 Civil Rights Act received its greatest opposition from members of the Democratic Party. The law was designed to establish a Civil Rights Commission and permit the government to bring lawsuits for various civil rights violations, including the denial of the right to vote.

William Winstead, a Democrat from Mississippi argued that: *"This bill contains most of the evil provisions of last year's so-called civil rights bill, plus an additional section which would empower the Attorney General of the United States to seek injunctions in the Federal district court for the enforcement of alleged violations of civil rights laws."*

Richard Russell, the Democratic senator from Georgia, argued:

"This law will be administered by a politically minded Attorney General. There can be little doubt that he will be constantly pressed by the Vice President of the United States [Richard Nixon] to apply the great powers of the law in the

*Southern States, at such places and in such time and manner as the **NAACP, of which the Vice President is the most distinguished member**, may demand.*

The threat of this vicious legislation will be used to intimidate honest officials of the state and local governments who are earnestly endeavoring to discharge their duties under their oaths of the office and <u>the laws of their respective States</u>.

It is entirely likely that the application of this law will result in <u>forcing the registration of a large number of Negro citizens</u> who, in fact, cannot meet the qualifications prescribed for all electors under the laws of the State in which they live. It is a thoroughly bad bill, and places dangerous powers in the hands of those who are to administer it without much comforting proof of their responsibility and fairness.

In the Senate, opponents were successful in eliminating Part III of the bill, which was aimed at striking down the separation of the races in hospitals, in schools, in hotels, at swimming pools, and in places of public entertainment. Senator Russell went on to say, *"As I have said, the bill is bad, but consider how much worse it would have been if we had not been able to eliminate Part III.*

"If the original Part III had been applied so as to bring about the social intermingling of the races from the kindergarten to the grave, southern civilization would have been destroyed beyond hope of redemption. This was the supreme tragedy we sought above all else to avert."

William Colmer, a Democratic congressman from Mississippi said, *"Some of us have conscientiously and therefore stubbornly opposed this misnamed civil-rights proposal. It is nothing more or less than the abolition of the Civil Rights of all the people under the guise of granting civil rights to a highly organized and politically powerful minority group.*

So, Mr. Speaker, as we gather today in this historic Chamber to witness the final act in the tragedy of the beginning of the downfall of the Republic, it might be well to briefly sum up the value of the winners and losers in this political gamble.

*"The actors in this political tragedy are of the summit stature in both political camps. It is obvious that the Republican high command has deliberately set out to recapture the minority Negro vote stolen from them by the **Democratic** high command some two decades ago."*

Senator Clifford Case, a Republican from New Jersey, argued, *"Mr. President, the facts, which have been developed in debate in the House and in the Senate, indicated clearly the deprivation of voting rights that exist in this country and the need for further legislation for the enforcement of those rights…. It is particularly appropriate, Mr. President, that these further remedies be by the way of preventive relief. As I indicated earlier, it does not do a person who has been deprived of his right to vote any good to have the person who deprives him of the right, put in jail, and no amount of money damages can compensate a person deprived of the right to vote for that deprivation. In spite of the existence of these theoretical remedies, the right to vote has been taken <u>away from millions of our citizens</u>. It is clear that an additional remedy is required."*

Debates took place June 5-18, 1957 in the House and August 29-30 in the Senate.

1960
Black Students Stage a "Sit-in"

On February 1, 1960, Joseph McNeil, Franklin McCain, David Richmond, and Ezell Blair from North Carolina A&T went to the local F.W. Woolworth store in Greensboro, North Carolina, and were refused service. Disappointed with the store's racist policies, they launched our nation's first *"sit-in"* protest. When word spread of their protest, other students joined them. Local Democratic officials were angry that these black students would deliberately defy their laws of segregation and responded by arresting them.

1960
Democrats Who Opposed the
1960 Civil Rights Act

On February 5, 1960, Republican President, Dwight D. Eisenhower sent to Congress a message requesting that: *"legislation to strengthen the law dealing with obstruction of justice so as to provide expressly that the use of force or threats of force to obstruct court orders in school desegregation cases shall be a federal offense."* He said, *"There have been instances where* [Democrat] *extremists have attempted, by mob violence and other concerted threats of violence, to obstruct the accomplishment of objectives in school decrees."*

Like the 1957 Civil Rights Act, this bill had **bi-partisan** support. But there were still Democrats that opposed the bill. In his argument **for** the bill, **Democratic Congressman Ray Madden of Indiana** said, *"Patriotic Negroes of America only ask that their future generations are not called upon to combat the economic and educational impediments which their ancestors endured."*

Congressman Overton Brooks, a Democrat from Louisiana, countered and argued that, *"This Civil Rights bill is as vicious an instrument as I have read since I have been in this Congress. If enacted into law, it will undoubtedly hurt our people in the South. The bill provides that anybody who writes a letter critical of a decree of the Federal courts dealing with the integration of schools, with the intent to obstruct the execution of an order of this court, is guilty of* *a Federal crime and punishable by fine and imprisonment. The provision regarding fleeing from one State to another to avoid prosecution or imprisonment for the crime of bombing or setting fire to a building, whether it be church or otherwise, makes another step toward taking away from States their fundamental rights. "*

Congressman William McCulloch, a Republican from Ohio, argued, *"For almost a century, the failure to provide political equality for all qualified citizens has been nagging the conscience of the people, and now we are obliged to consider and pass legislation to insure and implement such rights to all qualified citizens, which rights so long ago, were extended to all, only to be lost or taken away, in a substantial number of states or lesser political subdivision of our country."*

1960
Why Kennedy Was Reluctant to Help Dr. King

The 1960's was a turbulent time. It was a time of a hotly contested presidential campaign between Nixon and Kennedy and it was a time when the tension between blacks and whites was at an all-time high. Like most candidates, Kennedy wanted the black vote but not at the expense of losing the southern white Democratic vote. According to Kennedy's Civil Rights Advisor, Harris Wofford – Governor Vandiver, Griffin Bell, and other Democratic white supporters had told Kennedy that he would *"lose Georgia and several other states"* if he interfered or issued a strong statement protesting Dr. King's arrest in Georgia because *"the state of Georgia and its **Democratic governor** were parties to King's imprisonment."* In his book, *Of Kennedys and Kings: Making Sense of the Sixties*, Wofford says, M*uch has been made of Kennedy's actions and Nixon's inaction while Martin King was in a Georgia jail in October 1960. The impact on*

Fearing that he would lose the southern Democratic vote, Kennedy was angry when he learned that a key member of his staff intervened to get Dr. King released from the Georgia jail.

black voters and on the electoral votes has been analyzed and reported. But the full story of the reactions of John and Robert Kennedy and of Coretta, Martin, and Daddy King has not been told" (14-23). Wofford goes on to say that it was he who called to get King released, not John F. Kennedy, and because of that call, King was not only released, but Daddy King (Martin's father) publicly announced that he would now support Kennedy instead of Nixon. Daddy King was led to believe that it was Kennedy that had made the called to get his son out of jail. The full story is that, fearing that he would lose the white (southern) Democratic vote, Kennedy and his key advisors were quite upset when they learned that Wofford had called on his (Kennedy's) behalf. Strategically, Wofford found a way for the Kennedys to take advantage of the situation without revealing the fact that Kennedy never made the call and without loosing the white southern Democratic vote. After Daddy King's endorsement, blacks across the country gave Kennedy their support.

1961
Freedom Riders Beaten
in Democratic Controlled South

In 1961, the Student Nonviolent Coordinating Committee and the Congress of Racial Equality participated in Freedom Rides to challenge segregated restrooms, restaurants, and other facilities in the Democratic-controlled south. In Anniston, Alabama, Freedom Riders were beaten, and a white mob destroyed their bus by fire. In Montgomery, Alabama, when James Zwerg, a white Freedom Rider, was severely beaten, the town's ambulance service refused to take him to the hospital. Local Democratic officials responded by arresting those participating in the Freedom Rides—but not those who assaulted them.

1962
New Democratic Governor Pledges
Segregation Forever

In 1962, George C. Wallace was elected governor of Alabama. During his inaugural speech, the Democratic governor issued the following pledge: *"In the name of the greatest people that have ever trod this earth, I draw the line in the dust and toss the gauntlet before the feet of tyranny, and I say segregation now, segregation tomorrow, and segregation forever."*

1962
James Meredith Escorted to School
by U.S. Marshals

In September of 1962, after Democratic governor, Ross Barnett declared that *"we will never surrender to the evil and illegal forces of tyranny,"* he personally turned James Meredith away from registering as a first black student of the University of Mississippi. Meredith was escorted by John Doar and James McShane, two U.S. Marshals. Once Meredith was brought onto campus, Democratic officials ordered the Mississippi highway patrolmen to abandon their post, and violence broke out. Federal troops were brought in to quell the violence.

1963
Attack on Blacks Ordered by City Officials

In 1963, city officials of Birmingham, Alabama (with the blessings of Democratic Governor George Wallace), ordered the use of clubs, police dogs, and high pressured fire hoses to disburse a crowd of civil rights protestors. When their brutal, inhumane acts were captured on national and international television, the president was embarrassed. Four hundred civil rights protestors were arrested.

With the sanction of local and state Democratic officials, thousands of blacks were beaten and arrested by local and state law enforcement officers.

1963
Governor Blocks Registration of Black Students

In 1963, Democratic governor, George Wallace carried out his pledge to maintain segregation by defying a presidential order to register two black students in the state's university. The governor relented only after President Kennedy federalized the Alabama National Guard to assist in the matter.

1963
NAACP Field Secretary Murdered

In 1963, thirty-seven-year-old Medgar Evers, the NAACP's field secretary of Jackson, Mississippi, was assassinated on the front porch of his home. Local Democrats were pleased to learn of his death and believed this act of terrorism would re-emphasize the need for blacks to stay in their place.

1963
March on Washington Not Supported by the President

On August 28, 1963, the largest Civil Rights demonstration ever seen of modern times took place in Washington, D.C. Because of the racial tension in the nation, President Kennedy and Attorney General Robert Kennedy did not think the march was a good idea and chose not to participate. When John Lewis, a Freedom Rider who had been beaten in previous demonstrations took the microphone to speak, he attacked the Democratic Party for what he called their *"split personality"* on race and demanded that they take action. Congressman John Lewis is now a powerful member of Congress and one of the contributors in the book that covered lynchings in the Democrat-controlled south. The book, *Without Sanctuary* was the same book that inspired Senate Resolution 39 in 2005. The Resolution condemned past lynchings.

1963
Birmingham Bombing Kills Four Black Girls

Three weeks after the march on Washington, four young black girls were killed while attending Sunday school at the 16th Street Baptist Church, when a bomb exploded. It was not surprising in a city controlled by Democratic officials that no one was convicted of this horrible crime. Convictions came thirty-nine years later when President George W. Bush had the case reopened. In 2002, Bobby Cherry was arrested and convicted for the bombing (by a Republican administration).

1963
Democratic Administration Approves
Wiretaps on King

In October of 1963, Attorney General Robert Kennedy gave FBI Director, J. Edgar Hoover permission to maintain a wiretap on King's home telephone. In December of 1963, the FBI's Domestic Intelligence Division held a nine-hour session that resulted in a secret program to discredit King. The surveillance program exposed Dr. King's extra-marital affairs but did not determine or confirm that he was a communist, which was the principle reason why the wiretaps were approved.

1964
Officials Covered-up the Murder
of Three Civil Rights Workers

Three civil rights workers from the north were killed in Mississippi while assisting blacks with voter registration.

Local Democratic officials, including the mayor, sheriff, and the deputy of Neshoba County conspired to cover up the murders. The victims were James Chaney, Michael Schwerner, and Andrew Goodman.

1964
Democrats' Opposition to 1964 Civil Rights Act

Two of the prime sponsors and supporters of this bill were Republican Senator Everett Dirksen of Illinois and Democratic Senator Hubert Humphrey of Minnesota who said, *"It is my desire to work in the closest relationship with our colleagues on the Republican side of the aisle. I do not consider the bill before us to be a Democratic bill or a Republican bill."* However the strongest opposition to this bill came from Humphrey's fellow Democrats. The law, which contained eleven different titles, prohibited discrimination in all public accommodations, if their operation *"affected commerce including: hotels and other places of lodging of more than five rooms, restaurants and other eating places, gasoline stations, theaters, motion picture houses, stadiums and other places of exhibitions or entertainment."* It also included *voting, desegregation of public education, equal opportunity, and a Civil Rights Commission.* This bill was almost identical to the 1875 Civil Rights Act that the Democrats successfully had the United States Supreme Court reject and declare as *"unconstitutional."*

Background Leading Up to 1964 Civil Rights Act

In his book, *Why We Can't Wait*, Dr. Martin Luther King said, *"the feeling was growing among Negroes that the* [Kennedy] *administration had oversimplified and underestimated the civil rights issue.... The administration had fashioned its primary approach to discrimination in the South.... With each new Negro protest we were advised* [by the administration], *sometimes privately and sometimes in public, to call off our efforts and channel all of our energies into registering voters.* *On each occasion we would agree with the importance of voting rights, but would patiently seek to explain that Negroes did not want to neglect all other rights while one was selected for concentrated attention. The Kennedy administration appeared to believe it had, by its positive deeds, earned enough credit to coast on civil rights....”*

King went on to say, *“no one would have ever believed that during the first two years of the Kennedy administration”* (1961-1962) that Negroes *“would become as militant as the segregationists.”*

What King was referring to was the social unrest that African Americans vehemently expressed during the first two years of the Kennedy administration.

❖ In 1961, Freedom Riders were attacked and arrested in the south and blacks protested. Robert Kennedy ordered six hundred Federal marshals to Montgomery, Alabama, to maintain order.

❖ In 1962, several thousand federal troops were ordered to the University of Mississippi to maintain order as riots erupted when whites protested the admission of James Meredith, a twenty-nine-year-old black veteran.

❖ In 1962, black churches in Georgia were burned to discourage voter registration.

❖ In 1963, the nation was in chaos; the situation was out of control. By the week of May 18, the Department of Justice had noted that there had been **forty-three** different civil rights demonstrations of various magnitudes. On 3rd of April, Dr. King demonstrated in Birmingham, Alabama. The numbers of demonstrators increased significantly by 3rd of May. There were more demonstrations after Medgar Evers, (a civil rights leader) was assassinated in Mississippi. By May 7th, over twenty-five hundred demonstrators had been arrested, many of them children. On May 11th, a black leader's home was bombed. During that same period, **Democratic** governor, George Wallace, refused to comply with a presidential order to register two black students for classes at the University of Alabama; and four black children were killed when the 16th Street Baptist Church was bombed. The four young girls who were victims of the bombing were all personal friends of Condoleezza Rice, our current Secretary of State (2008). All of the aforementioned atrocities took place in states controlled by Democrats.

In his book, *The Statutory History of the United States*, Professor Bernard Schwartz states: *"The events in Birmingham, followed by the need to federalize the Alabama National Guard to frustrate George Wallace, the Democratic Governor of Alabama, whose efforts to thwart a court order admitting two Negro students to the state university, roused the national conscience, as almost never before, to the need for speedy action to correct the situation. Most important perhaps, they stimulated a previously lukewarm Administration to becoming firm supporters of strong civil rights legislation. The tepid attitude of President John Kennedy in the matter had been a source of serious discomfort to many of his supporters... The troubles in Alabama completely altered the Administration's attitude to make a full commitment to civil rights that, he had until then, so carefully avoided"* (*Statutory History of the United States* Vol 2, 1017)

On June 19, 1963, President Kennedy sent the following letter to Congress, asking Congress to pass his 1963 Civil Rights Bill. The first section of the letter seems to suggest that the president was more concerned with the social disorder that was taking place, than he was about the deplorable conditions of the African Americans.

President Kennedy's Message to Congress
For Passage of 1963 Civil Rights Act
June 19, 1963

Last week I addressed to the American people an appeal to conscience – a request for their cooperation in meeting the growing moral crisis in American race relations. I warned of "a rising tide of discontent that threatens the public safety" in many parts of the country. I emphasized that the events in Birmingham and elsewhere have so increased the cries for equality that no city or state or legislative body can prudently choose to ignore them. "It is a time to act," I said, "in the Congress, in State and local legislative bodies and, above all, in all of our daily lives.

*In the days that have followed, the predictions of **increased violence** have been tragically borne out. The "fires of frustration and discord" have burned hotter than ever.*

At the same time, the response of the American people to this appeal to their principles and obligations has been reassuring. Private progress – by merchants and the unions and local organizations – has been marked, if not uniform, in many areas. Many doors long closed to Negroes, North and South, have been opened. Local biracial committees, under private and public sponsorship, have mushroomed. The mayors of our major cities, whom I earlier addressed, have pledged renewed action. But persisting inequalities and tensions make it clear that Federal action must lead the way, providing both the Nation's standard and a nationwide solution. In short, the time has come for the Congress of the United States to join with the executive and judicial branches in making it clear to all, that race has no place in American life or law...

The result of continued Federal legislative inaction will be continued, if not increased, racial strife – causing the leadership on both sides to pass from the hands of reasonable responsible men to the purveyors of hate and violence, endangering domestic tranquility, retarding our nation's economic and social progress, and weakening the respect with which the rest of the world regards us. No American, I feel sure, would prefer this course of tension, disorder, and division – and the great majority of our citizens simply cannot accept it.

For these reasons, I am proposing that Congress stay in session this year until it has enacted – preferably as a single omnibus bill – the most responsible, reasonable, and urgently needed solutions to this problem, solutions which should be acceptable to all fair-minded men. This bill would be known as the Civil Rights Act of 1963....

President Kennedy died before the bill was passed, and his successor, President Lyndon Johnson, had a difficult time convincing his own party that such legislation was necessary. <u>Because of the strong opposition by Southern Democrats</u>, the debates involving this bill lasted over eighty days. The debates took up some seven thousand pages in the Congressional Record (consisting of over ten million words) and created the longest filibuster in Senate history, led by the senior Democratic senator from Tennessee, Al Gore Sr. The following are a few of the Democrats who opposed the 1964 Civil Rights Act and the Republicans who supported it.

In his arguments against the bill, **Donald Matthews, of Florida** said, *"In the name of Civil Rights, this bill would deprive schoolchildren of milk and basic education if there appears to be discrimination because of race, color, or national origin. How cruel can the humanitarians and the moralists be in the name of Civil Rights? What do we mean by discrimination? The communists have been fed under Republican and Democratic administrations, but this will deny daily bread to American children in the name of Civil Rights."*

Thomas Abernethy, a Democrat from Mississippi, argued, *"If enacted, it is certain to precipitate a tremendous upheaval in our society, but not the kind of upheaval that proponents* *apparently expect. I predict it will precipitate an upheaval that will make the sit-ins, kneel-ins, lie-ins, mass picketing, chanting, the march on Washington, and all other elements of the **so-called Negro revolutions**, all of these – I predict – will look like kindergarten play in comparison with the counter-revolution that is bound to arise and continue to grow, and grow, and grow."*

Howard Smith, a Democrat from Virginia, added: *"I deeply regret that out of the 15 minutes allotted to me, I cannot assign time for protest to the many patriotic members of this House who would like to express their distaste, dismay, and disgust at this invasion of the rights of American citizens. In a few minutes, you will vote this monstrous instrument of oppression upon all of the American People.... **Be forewarned that the paid agents and leaders of the NAACP** can never permit this law to be gradually and peacefully accepted because that means an end to their well-paid activities."*

Democratic Senator Robert Byrd of West Virginia argued, *"Can the Senator from Minnesota [Humphrey] assure the Senator from West Virginia that under Title VI school children may not be bused from one end of the community to another end of the community at the taxpayers' expense to relieve so-called racial imbalance in the schools?"*

Democrat Sam Ervin added, *"This bill is based upon a strange thesis. The thesis is that the best way and the only way to promote the civil rights of some Americans is to rob all Americans of civil rights equally precious, and to reduce the supposedly sovereign states to meaningless zeros on the nation's map."*

Senator Olin Johnston, a Democrat from South Carolina, said, *"Mr. President, this is indeed the blackest day in the <u>U.S. Senate since 1875,</u> when the Congress passed a civil rights bill* *similar to this one. It was 89 years ago that the* [Republican] *Congress passed the nefarious Reconstruction era civil rights laws, <u>identical with what we are now discussing, which were later declared unconstitutional by the U.S. Supreme Court</u>. The Senate, if it passes this measure before us, will be compounding that unconstitutional error made back in 1875* [when the Republicans passed the 1875 Civil Rights Act]. *I predict that this bill will never be enforced without turning our nation into a police state and without the cost of bloodshed and violence.*

"Ten years ago, in 1954, the Supreme Court took it upon itself to amend the Constitution of the United States and declared that segregation – that is, required separate but equal school facilities for the races – was illegal. Instead of promoting peace and harmony between the races, as a result of this decision we have seen racial violence, intolerance, bigotry, and hatred compounded and multiplied. Whenever Government decrees a social policy for people when people are not behind such a policy, one can only expect as a result such violence and trouble.

"Those who advocate passage of this civil rights bill need not expect this legislation to do anything for our country except to divide our people and rekindle the hatreds and prejudices of 100 years ago, to be perpetuated into the future for at least another 100 years. Contained in this legislation is not just a so-called framework for engendering equality among people of different races. This bill contains the equipment, tools, temptation and power to establish a vast Federal network for controlling the people of every community. The damage this will do to our Government is incomprehensible....

"When one talks of eliminating discrimination with this piece of so-called legislation, if it were not such a serious matter, it would be fit for a good joke....

"If we sweep away the clutter of emotion and the clatter of the demonstrators and look at the legal aspect of this legislation, we can only come to the realistic conclusion that it is unconstitutional and will be recorded in history as the greatest robber of the rights of individuals and States and the most tremendous hoax ever perpetrated upon the people of the United States."

Senator John Sparkman, a Democrat from Alabama, told the Senate, *"Mr. President, we now have before us a motion to proceed with the consideration of H.R. 7152, the so-called civil rights bill....*

"Mr. President, never in my long history of opposition to so-called civil rights legislation have I risen to attack so formidable an array of legislation that is probably well-intended but which could do so much to take away many of the liberties and rights for which we have fought throughout the history of this Nation....

"...For months I have been receiving literally thousands of letters from all over the nation supporting my stand against this bill. So I rise not just with a mandate from the people of Alabama, or the South. My mandate comes from the four corners of the country....

"Title II, the so-called public accommodations provision of H.R. 7152, is the most sweeping, the most far-reaching attempt to repeal the constitutional concept of individual liberty that has been proposed since the cruel period of [the Republican's] *Reconstruction.*

"In those days, when the Southland lay prostrate, crushed, harshly ruled by military governors [appointed by the Republicans], *the Congress, in which the South was misrepresented in many cases by residents of Northern States, rammed through the* [Republican's] *notorious **Civil Rights Act***

of 1875. *This was one of the infamous 'force bills' designed to tear apart the very fabric of southern life.*

"Fortunately for the Nation, those aggrieved had recourse to the Constitution. Even though amended under questionable circumstances, the Constitution was our salvation because when [the Democrats challenged the issue in court] *and the Supreme Court put the Civil Rights of 1875 to the ultimate test, it was found wanting.*

"Mr. President, I for one, am going to devote my best efforts to returning this resurrected [Republican] *statute to its grave."*

Senator Everett Dirksen, Illinois Republican, addressed the Senate, urging his *"fellow Senators to consider this issue in the light of national interest. It is a phrase that came close to the late President Kennedy. It is a phrase that comes close to our former majority leader, who now occupies his exalted position. I want to do what I think is in the interest of the present and future wellbeing of probably the only real, true free republic that still remains on God's footstool. I shall cooperate. I shall do my best...."*

<u>Emanuel Celler, Democrat from New York,</u> was one of the Democrats that argued in favor of the bill. Celler said, *"This is an opportunity for which we have been anxiously awaiting. You know, the Lord's best gifts to us are not things, but opportunities, and we now have bestowed upon us a golden opportunity to do a great thing.*

"Both parties joined hands. We felt we represented a cause. We shunned a political issue. I am grateful to the ranking member of the Republican Party on the Judiciary Committee, the gentleman from Ohio [Mr. McCulloch]. *He and I labored incessantly fashioning the bill. I pay tribute to him and his fellow Republicans who stood by him.... The demonstration and violence of the recent months have served to point up*

Blacks were consistently terrorized in southern states, counties, towns and cities that were under the jurisdiction of Democratic officials.

what many of us have known for years: That this nation can no longer abide the moral outrage of discrimination."

William McCullough, Republican from Ohio, followed with these comments: *"No Statutory law can completely end discrimination under attack by this legislation. Intelligent work and vigilance by members of all races will be required for many years, before discrimination completely disappears. To create hope of immediate and complete success can only promote conflict and result in brooding and despair. No force or fear, then, but belief in the inherent equality of man induces me to support this legislation.*

"I believe in the right of each individual to have his constitutional rights guaranteed. On the other hand, he must always be prepared to shoulder the obligations and assume the burdens of citizenship.

No one would suggest that the Negro receives equality of treatment and equality of opportunity in many fields of activity, today. Well-informed persons, everywhere, admit that in all sections of the country – North, South, East, and West – the Negro continues to face the barriers of racial intolerance and discrimination. Hundreds of thousands of citizens are denied the basic right to vote. Thousands of school districts remain segregated. Decent hotel and eating accommodations frequently lie hundreds of miles apart for the Negro traveler. Parks, playgrounds, and golf courses continue to be off limits to Negroes whose tax money go to support them. Many programs continue to be operated in a discriminatory manner. These, and many more such conditions, point the way toward the need for additional legislation. I recommend H.R. 7152, as amended, to all my colleagues from wheresoever they come."

By the time this bill passed, the damage had already been done, millions of blacks had been murdered, mutilated, burned to death, bombed, forced to work in prison labor camps and had been enslaved for over 250 years in states controlled by Democrats. It was a step in the right direction, but 250 years and several million deaths too late.

1965
Violence in the Democratic Controlled South Continues

One year after the passage of the 1964 Civil Rights Act, **Democratic** Governor, George Wallace, of Alabama, ordered two hundred State Troopers and members of the Dallas County Sheriff's office to stop more than five hundred civil rights marchers. Seventeen blacks were hospitalized and sixty-seven others were treated for injuries from night sticks, tear gas, and whips.

1965
Members of Democratic Party Oppose Voting Rights

The debates on 1965 Voting Rights Act began with a speech from the Democratic President, Lyndon B. Johnson. On March 15, 1965, he delivered the following address to the Congress of the United States. (The following are excerpts of his speech.)

Mr. Speaker, Mr. President, Members of the Congress, I speak tonight for the dignity of man and the destiny of democracy. ...In our time we have come to live with moments of great crisis. Our lives have been marked with debate about great issues; issues of war and peace, of prosperity and depression. But rarely in any time does an issue lay bare the secret heart

*of America itself.... The issue of equal rights for American
Negroes is such an issue. And should we defeat every enemy,
should we double our wealth and conquer the stars, and still
be unequal to this issue, then we will have failed as a people
and as a nation. For with a country as with a person, what is
a man profited if he shall gain the whole world and lose his
own soul?*

*...To deny a man his hopes because of his color or race, his
religion, or place of birth – is not only to do injustice, it is to
deny America and to dishonor the dead who gave their lives
for American freedom. ...Yet the harsh fact is that in many
places in this country, men and women are kept from voting
because they are Negroes... All Americans must have the right
to vote, and we are going to give that right.*

*"...Above the pyramid on the great seal of the United States
its says – in Latin – 'God has favored our undertaking.'
God will not favor everything we do. It is rather our duty
to divine His will. But I cannot help believing that He truly
understands and that He really favors the undertaking that
we begin here tonight." (Statutory History, 1506-1510)*

With bipartisan support, the debates to eliminate voting
irregularities in the Democratic controlled south started on
April 22, 1965. The newly proposed bill called for providing
congressional enforcement of the 15th Amendment in the
election process.

Several participated in the debate, but the primary persons
who controlled the debates were Republican Senators
Everett Dirksen of Illinois and Jacob Javits from New York
and Democratic Senators Sam Ervin of North Carolina and
Herman Talmadge of Georgia.

Sam Erivin: *"This bill contains a provision which condemns without judicial* trial [most of the Democrats' southern states including] *the States of Alabama, Mississippi, Louisiana, Georgia, South Carolina and Virginia and 34 counties in North Carolina; does it not?"*

Senator Dirksen: *"Yes; I do not believe it condemns the States. It takes account of a condition that has existed in those States. We are seeking to remedy a condition that exists with respect to citizens of the United States. We go to the heart of the problem and seek to supply a remedy that we think is constitutional and non-punitive."*

Herman Talmadge, Democrat from Georgia: *"We were told last year that with the passage of a broad, all-encompassing civil rights bill, which covered almost everything that the mind of man could conceive, that there would not be any further need of a civil rights bill. Would not the bill deny to the* [Democratic] *States of Louisiana, Alabama, Mississippi, Georgia, North Carolina, and certain carefully selected counties in other areas the right to apply any literacy standards whatsoever for their voters?"*

Regarding literacy test, **Republican Senator Jacob Javits** responded: *"Think of the situation, for example in Mississippi, where whites are asked to interpret the following provision of the State Constitution: 'The Senate shall consist of Members chosen every 4 years by the qualified electors of the several districts.' Negroes are asked to interpret sections of the Constitution dealing with tax exemptions, the judicial sale of land, eminent domain, concurrent jurisdiction of chancery and circuit courts and habeas corpus. [And] What about deprivation going back for a century, which occurred in segregated schools, resulting in a median education level of the sixth grade for Negroes in Mississippi, as compared*

*with an 11th grade median for whites? Then there is the
intimidation by public officials; there are the bombings and
shooting, the burnings, the beatings; and quite apart from
them, the denial of surplus food to Negroes who persist in their
attempt to register, as in Humphreys County, Mississippi; or
the boycotting of Negroes who had the temerity to register by
cutting off their bank loans and their grocery store credit."*

The passage of this bill was a major defeat for the southern
Democrats who eventually changed courses after the
registration of millions of black voters. It was only after these
successful voter registration drives did the Democratic Party
start to consistently court the black vote. As the saying goes,
"if you can't beat them, join them."

A few years earlier, Lyndon B. Johnson had put it another
way. He told Richard B. Russell of Georgia: *"These Negroes,
they're getting pretty uppity these days and that's a problem
for us since they got something now that they never had
before, the political pull to back up their uppityness. Now
we've got to do something about this, we've got to give **them
a little something, just enough to quiet them down, not
enough to make a difference.** For if we don't move at all,
then their allies will line up against us and there'll be no way
of stopping them, we'll lose the filibuster and there'll be no
way of putting a brake on **all sorts of wild legislation.** It'll
be Reconstruction all over again."* Quote taken from Doris
Kearns Goodwin's book entitled: Lyndon Johnson and the
American Dream page 148.

1966
Another Racist Democrat Elected Governor

In 1966, Lester Maddox was elected as the new Democratic
Governor for the state of Georgia. Maddox was the business

owner who was known for chasing away black customers with his pistol, distributing ax handles to patrons as an anti-integration tool, and for closing his fried chicken restaurant in Atlanta to avoid compliance with the 1964 Civil Rights Act.

1968
Some Democrats Oppose 1968 Civil Rights Act

The *bi-partisan* bill was designed to protect Negroes and civil-rights workers by outlawing racially-motivated acts of violence against persons exercising their rights under the 14th Amendment. It also had a fair housing component to ban discrimination in housing.

Democrats opposing the 1968 Civil Rights Act included Lawrence Fountain and Sam Ervin, Democrats from North Carolina. **Fountain said,** *"If this bill becomes law, it will be a clear invitation to this tiny band of agitators to continue to foment strife and fuel civil disorder. We have seen too much of that lately and why we seem to want to nourish it, is beyond me. But that is exactly what the impact of this bill would be."*

Sam Ervin said, *"It would be easy to defeat their efforts if they were evil-minded men professing bad ends. Unfortunately for the cause of sound constitutional government, however, they are men of good intentions who are willing to do constitutional evil because they believe good will result from it. In so doing, they emulate the example of Mother Eve, who succumbed to the temptation to eat the forbidden fruit because she saw 'it was pleasant to the eyes,' and believed it to be 'good for food,' and was satisfied that it 'would make one wise.'*

"The men who seek to destroy or impair these constitutional principles and constitutional rights claim that it is necessary for the federal government to deprive all Americans of basic

economic, legal personal and property rights to give equality to 20 million Negro Americans."

John Stennis, the Democrat from Mississippi said, *"I wish to be clear that I oppose this measure in most of its major particulars, and that I have been one of many who have worked to avoid it. I believe particularly with reference to the passage of the open housing legislation, that it will prove to be a grave mistake and **one of the gravest that the Senate has ever made."***

1971
The Name "Democrat" Removed from Black Caucus

In January 1969, newly elected African American representatives of the 77th Congress joined six incumbents to form the *"Democratic Select Committee."* In 1971, after a recommendation from one of its members, the word *"Democratic"* was removed from the organization's name, and the African American political group was renamed the *"Congressional Black Caucus."* Some speculate that perhaps the recommendation was made because members of the caucus were well aware of the Democrats' racist past and wanted to distance themselves from their racist history. Others claim that the organization merely wanted to stay politically neutral, even though they all ran on a Democratic ticket.

1972
Opposition to the 1972 Equal Employment Act

The Purpose of the bill was to assure and promote equal opportunity in employment. The voting record on this piece of legislation shows that even though the Democratic Party was gaining more of the black vote, there were still Democrats who opposed equality for blacks. Congressional records reveal that 155 Democrats voted for the bill and 79 voted against it. On the Republican side of the isle 130 Republicans voted for it and 26 voted against it.

This bill was passed during the Nixon Administration. Shortly after the passage of this bill, Nixon issued Executive Order 11246 and 11478 which paved the way for Affirmative Action programs, a program that included quotas, goals, and timetables. Nixon's 1972 Equal Employment Opportunities Act granted EEOC power to bring *"Pattern and Practice"* lawsuits in discrimination cases.

1973
Democrat Elect First Black from South

One hundred and eighty-one (181) years after the Democratic Party was originally formed (1792) and almost one decade after the passage of the 1964 Civil Rights Act, Barbara Jordan became the Democrats' *first black* member of Congress from the South.

1983
Obama Talks about Racist Democrats
in Chicago

In his best selling book: *Dreams from My Father*, Obama shares a conversation between blacks while visiting a local barbershop in Chicago. He documents this conversation regarding blacks and their relationship with Chicago Democrats on pages 147-148 of the book.

During the conversation, one man referred to the period before Harold Washington was elected as Chicago's first black mayor – as: *"Plantation politics."* A man named Smithy responded: *"That's just what it was too. A Plantation. Black people in the worst jobs. The worst housing. Police brutality rampant. But when the so-called black committeemen came around election time, we'd all line up and vote the straight Democratic ticket. Sell our soul for a Christmas turkey. White folks spitting in our faces and we'd reward them with the vote."* They went on to discuss how difficult it was to elect a black mayor in Chicago. One customer remembered how blacks rallied around their black candidate when *"white Democratic Committeemen, Vrdolyak and others* [white Democrats], *announced their support for the Republican candidate, saying that the city would go to hell if it had a black mayor."* After hearing that white Democrats vowed to vote for a Republican before they would vote for a black mayor, the customer said, *"blacks turned out in record numbers* to elect Washington.

2001
Blacks Lose Land in Democratic
Controlled States

On December 2, 2001, the Associated Press reported that in southern states and counties (controlled by Democrats), black Americans who owned fifteen million acres of farmland in 1910, now own only 2.2 million. The AP reporters said many blacks lost their land through cheating, intimidation, and even murder. In order to cover up these injustices, many southern courthouses were burned to the ground to destroy the evidence.

2004
Blacks File Reparation Lawsuit against
Democrats

In 2004, a class action reparation lawsuit was filed (by the author of this book) on behalf of all African Americans. The lawsuit demanded a public apology from the Democratic

Party for its past racist practices. The Democratic National Committee and its leadership refused to apologize and hired a prestigious law firm to represent them.

2005
Democrats' Connection with the Katrina Disaster

Everyone agrees that the federal response to Katrina was too slow, but what they failed to recognize is that according to the New Orlean's Comprehensive Emergency Plan, the primary persons responsible for evacuating the city and providing shelters with food and water for the at-risk population, was Mayor Nagin (Democrat) and Governor Kathleen Blanco (Democrat), not the federal government (President Bush). The Plan does not mention a role for the federal government. The plan actually states: *"Authority to issue evacuations of elements of the population is vested in the Mayor...."* It further states in other sections of the plan that: *"Conduct of an actual evacuation will be the responsibility of the Mayor of New Orleans in coordination with the* [the city's] *Director of the Office of Emergency Preparedness (OEP)...."*

It was no secret that at-risk poor blacks who lived in the 9th Ward, lived in termite-infested and rat-infested homes that were susceptible and vulnerable to severe hurricanes and devastating floods. Historical records reveal that they had lived under these types of conditions since 1877 when Democrats (who wanted full control of the south), demanded that federal troops be removed from the south. In a letter dated, August 23, 1888, blacks from New Orleans complained about what it was like living under Democrat control (see letter on page 41).

2006
Democrats Refuse to Apologize
for Their Racist Past

On January 9, 2006, the following letter was sent to key members of the Democratic Party explaining why the 2004 lawsuit was filed. No one responded. Among those who received a copy of the letter was Senator Barack Obama.

from the office
of
Rev. Wayne Perryman

P.O. Box 256 Mercer Island, WA 98040 (206) 232-5575
Doublebro@aol.com

January 9, 2006

Congressional Black Caucus	National Bar Association
NAACP	National Urban League
Dr. Cornell West	Professor Charles Ogletree
Senator Hillary Clinton	Senator Joseph Biden
Senator Barack Obama	Senator Edward Kennedy
Senator Joseph Lieberman	Senator Barbara Boxer
Senator Pat Roberts	Senator Carl Levin
Senator Diane Feinstein	Cong. John Conyers
Cong. Jesse Jackson Jr.	Cong. Harold Ford
Senator Mary Landrieu	Senator Sam Brownback
Senator Bill Frist	Cong. Elijah Cummings

Attention Congressional & Community Leaders:

I thought it would only be fitting and proper to provide an explanation as to what brought about the Reparations lawsuit against the Democratic Party. Before I share with you the chain of events that led to the lawsuit, I thought that perhaps

I should give you a brief background on myself and my past political affiliation.

I am the author of several books, a former radio talk show host, a corporate consultant, a community activist and an inner-city minister located in Seattle Washington. In addition to working with gang members and professional athletes, I spend much of my leisure time doing research. In 1993, based on personal research, I challenged major Christian publishers and scholars that continued to produce publications promoting the *Curse of Ham* theory (a theory that justified slavery from a Christian perspective). My efforts resulted in a public apology and the removal of the 400-year-old *curse theory* from all of their publications including removing it from the *Encyclopedia Britannica* (see attached letters and articles). My book: *The 1993 Trial on the Curse of Ham* was based on that research.

Most of my adult life I have voted for and worked with a number of Democratic candidates at the local level. In 1996, I served as a member of the Washington State Black Clergy to Re-elect President Bill Clinton and worked closely with the co-chair. After President Clinton was re-elected, I was challenged by a group of young people from our church regarding the history of the Democratic Party and its relationship with blacks. Their challenge prompted me to devote a considerable amount of time researching the subject.

My research included reviewing Congressional Records from 1860 to present, reading the works of several renowned history professors (both black and white), and looking at the Democratic Platform from the early 1800's to 1954. In addition to these documents I reviewed the research of those who produced the books: *Without Sanctuary, 100 Years of Lynchings* and added to my library PBS and the History Channel's series on *The Rise and Fall of Jim Crow* and *Reconstruction: The Second Civil War*. Excerpts from those books and film documentaries were included as exhibits in my Reparations lawsuit against the Democratic Party.

The graphic depictions of whites fighting over the private parts of black men (penises, fingers, ears) after hanging them and igniting them with kerosene, is forever embedded in my mind. I can still hear the cries of the victims' wives and children pleading and begging for the lives of their loved ones while **Democratic** national and local elected officials joined the crowd and cheered. The lynching of Mary Turner, the nine-month-pregnant mother, was even more horrific and graphic. All of these events took place under the banner of **"States Rights"** in regions controlled by Democratic governors, mayors, judges, sheriffs, congressmen, and U.S. senators. Like Dr. King, my parents lived through those times in Atlanta, and I never fully appreciated what they and other blacks went through until I had completed my research.

In addition to lynchings and terrorist attacks by the Democrats' terrorist organizations (as revealed in the 1871 Senate hearings), Democrats legislated Black Codes, Jim Crow laws, and a multitude of other repressive legislation at the federal and state levels (and repealed other key pieces of civil rights legislation), all in an effort to deny blacks their rights as citizens. The entire system of racism in America was meticulously thought-out and carried out by a powerful political machine. And that political machine according to historians—was the Democratic Party— the party of *"White Supremacy."*

Based on these findings, I wrote my latest book, ***Unfounded Loyalty***, and sent the attached (November 7, 2004) letter to the DNC requesting that it issue an apology to African Americans. In 2005, I sent a second letter to the DNC, again requesting an apology. When the DNC ignored the first request, I filed my first lawsuit on December 10, 2004. Prior to my letters, members of the Congressional Black Caucus sent former Congressman J.C. Watts the attached letter (on January 28, 1999). In that letter the Caucus told Mr. Watts and his Republican counterparts to: *"Clearly and publicly distance themselves from the CCC and any other white supremacist, anti-semitic or hate groups...."* In my letter to the DNC, I expressed similar sentiments. I told the DNC *"An apology is one of the only ways modern-day Democrats can distance themselves from the party's racist past while bringing some closure to the African American Community."* Instead of apologizing, Howard Dean hired one of the most powerful law firms in the country to defend the party's racist past.

Without an apology and repentance, there is no way the Democratic Party can ***ever* sincerely** honor Dr. Martin Luther King Jr. and Ms. Rosa Parks, two individuals who literally gave their lives to destroy the racist programs, policies and practices that were established by the Democratic Party. And without an apology and repentance, there is no way the Democratic Party can ever respect African Americans. Its past programs and practices from slavery through Jim Crow, which literally destroyed the lives of ***millions*** of blacks, amounts to an **act of mass murder**. And to hire an attorney to defend that racist past is not only an official endorsement of murder—it is an insult to the entire black race and to those whites who gave their lives to eliminate racial injustice.

I look forward to your response.

Sincerely

Rev. Wayne Perryman

cc. Senator Maria Cantwell

2008
Clintons Accused of Racism

On May 26, 2008, allegations of racism within the Democratic Party continued when the New York Times reported that: *"The Clinton campaign began a concerted effort over the weekend to try to "set the record straight and contain the damage from Senator Hillary Roddam Clinton's comments' regarding what was perceived as a reference that something tragic might happen to Senator Barack Obama before the nomination is wrapped up in June. On Friday, May 23, 2008, Senator Clinton stated that she was staying the race because, "my husband did not wrap up the nomination in 1992 until he won the California primary.... We all remember Bobby Kennedy was assassinated in June in California."*

Kathy Kiely and Jill Lawrence, reporters for USA Today, implied that Senator Clinton made other racist statements when she argued that: *"She would be the stronger nominee because she appeals to a wider coalition of voters – including whites who have not supported Barack Obama in recent contests."* The article went on to say that Clinton cited an Associated Press article *"that found how Senator Obama's support among working – hardworking American, white Americans, is weakening again, and how whites in both states who had not completed college were supporting me."* Clinton when on to say, *"These are the people you have to win if you're a Democrat in sufficient numbers to actually win the election. Everybody knows that."* Blacks no longer feel that Bill Clinton was their first black President. A number of them now feel that he is no different from other southern Democrats who established the system of Jim Crow.

Many blacks believe the perceived racist comments from Senator Clinton and her husband is further evidence that racism still exist within the Democratic Party.

2008
Democrats' Past Racist Practices Ignored

Over the years, when the federal government launched various investigations to prosecute those who committed the racist acts outlined in this comprehensive analysis, elected officials from the Democratic Party including Democratic governors, judges, mayors, sheriffs, state legislators and United States Senators exhausted every means to block their investigations (as they did in the 2005 lawsuit, *African Americans v. National Democratic Party CV 05-00722-JCC*). Loyal members of the Democratic Party refused to cooperate in these federal investigations and with rare exceptions, fearful African Americans who were victims or witnessed these horrific atrocities - were too frightened to participate. The terrorist attacks inflicted by members of the Democratic Party and their Klan supporters (against blacks and white supporters of blacks) were so numerous, that many historians believe that from 1792 to the 1970's, this political party is responsible for killing and terrorizing more African Americans than the terrorist activities attributed to Osama Bin Laden, the Al Qaeda, the Baath Party and the Taliban of Afghanistan. Other historians suggest that the Nazi Party's agenda of *racial purity* may have been inspired by the Democratic Party's agenda of *racial supremacy*. The striking similarities between what happened to the Jews under the rule of Germany's Nazi Party versus what happened to blacks under the rule of the Democratic Party is worthy of academic and judicial review to determine whether or not an apology from the Democratic Party has merit.

On October 30, 2007, the Associated Press reported that the Rev. Al Sharpton demanded that Vice President Dick Cheney *"apologize"* and *"denounce"* the Clove Valley Rod and Gun

Club (which he, the Vice President had visited on October 29th). Sharpton pointed out that the club had displayed a Confederate flag inside one of its garages and that the flag *"represents lynchings, hate and murder to black people."* Eight years earlier (as stated before), on January 28, 1999, members of the Congressional Black Caucus sent former Congressman JC Watts a letter demanding that he and his Republican counterparts apologize and *"Clearly and publicly distance themselves from the CCC* [Council of Conservative Citizens] *and any other* [of what they perceive as] *white supremacist or hate groups."* It is important to note that although the Congressional Black Caucus and the Reverend Al Sharpton have consistently condemned groups and organizations with historical roots and ties to racism, they have yet to condemn the Democratic Party for their historical (200 year) racist past, nor have they ask the Party to apologize to blacks.

June 2008
Racist Democrats Still Members
of The Party Today

During a June 4, 2008, interview with Representative James Clyburn (Democrat), he told Foxnews radio that *his office has been deluged with nasty phone calls **with racial overtones** since his endorsement of Barack Obama. ... "* Clyburn went on to say, *"the **callers identified themselves as Hillary Clinton supporters**."* During the interview, he told how his white intern (who took the calls) was so upset *"that she had to be consoled by other workers and left the office early."*

"I was absolutely shocked," Clyburn continued, *"Could not believe that this happened. I could understand people saying. "Why are you doing this or why would you not support Hillary Clinton? But to call me the kinds of names I have not heard since the 40's and 50's? Some of the callers threatened to*

sabotage the election." Clyburn is the House Majority Whip and is considered to be the highest ranking African American in Congress.

In a June 5, 2008, article entitled: <u>Obama Heads to Election With Some Weakness</u>, reporter Amy Chozick of the Wall Street Journal said, *"The Illinois senator moves forward from the primaries after a string of losses"* and he goes with *"an apparent weakness in attracting **the white working class** demographic seen as crucial to the **Democratic** victory in November."* The facts clearly shows that contrary to what leading Democrats want us to believe, the racism that existed within the Democratic Party 200 years ago, is still alive and functioning today.

Clarification

The facts presented in this document are not to suggest or imply that every modern-day Democrat is a racist, nor is it the author's intent to suggest or imply that there were (or are) no racist Republicans, but rather to point out that as a party, during the past 150-plus years (historically), Republicans, as a party, never embraced or supported the kinds of racist practices and programs that the Democrats, as a party, established, supported, and endorsed. The facts are clear, the origins of racism in America had more to do with politics and power than it had to do with the entire white race.

Modern-day Republicans must learn from their predecessors who were sensitive enough to start the process of racial equality (for African Americans). They must pick up the mantle, embrace the principles of righteousness, and complete the job that their predecessors started.

Modern-day Democrats must stop pretending that they are the compassionate party of black people and confess that it was their predecessors who started many of the racist practices that we are now trying to eradicate.

Final Comments

Had Obama seized the opportunity to emphasize that **our nation** as a whole (meaning the collective white citizens of America) *never* endorsed slavery and that the roots of racism rested in the soil of his party, he would have narrowed what he called *"the chasm of misunderstanding that exists between the races."*

It is most unfortunate that Obama took the time to publicly denounce Rev. Jeremiah Wright's "wrong" statements, but he has never taken the time to publicly denounce his party's racist past which was far more devastating and divisive than his pastor's sermons or his grandmother's fears. My final two questions:

(1) If Obama was bold enough to resign from his church because of what they said about whites, will he be bold enough to resign from the Democratic Party because of what they did to blacks?

(2) Based on their horrific racist past as revealed in this comprehensive analysis, do Democrats owe African Americans an apology for supporting systems, programs, organizations, legislation and litigation that legally justified the death and destruction of millions of blacks during the past 200 years?

Appendix A

Democratic Attacks against Blacks in Kentucky

December 24, 1867   A colored schoolhouse was burned by incendiaries in Breckinridge.

January 28, 1868   Jim Macklin was taken from jail in Frankfort and hung.

May 28, 1868   Sam Davie was hung by a mob in Harrodsburg.

July 11, 1868   George Rogers was hung by a mob in Bradsfordsville, Martin County.

July 12, 1868   William Pierce was hung by a mob in Christian.

July 31, 1868   A colored school exhibition was attacked by a mob in Midway.

August 3, 1868   Cabe Fields was shot and killed by disguised men near Keen, Jessamine County.

August 7, 1868   Seven persons were ordered to leave their homes in Standford

August 1868   Silas Woodford, age sixty, badly beaten by disguised mob. Also beaten were Mary Smith Curtis and Margret Mosby near Keene, Jessemine County.

August 1868   James Gaines was expelled from Anderson by Ku Klux Klan.

August 1868   James Parker was killed by the Klan in Pulaski County.

August 1868	Noah Blankenship was whipped by a mob in Pulaski County.
August 1868	William Gibson and John Gibson hung by mob in Washington County.
August 21, 1868	Negroes attacked, robbed, and driven from Summerville.
August 28, 1868	F.H. Montford was hung by a mob near Cogers landing in Jessamine County.
September 1868	Negro hung by a mob.
September 1868	A U.S. Marshall named Meriwether was attacked, captured, and beaten to death by a mob in Larue County.
September 5, 1868	William Glassgow was killed by a mob in Warren County.
September 11, 1868	Two Negroes were beaten by Klan in Anderson County.
September 11, 1868	Oliver Stone's house was attacked by mob in Fayette County.
September 18, 1868	Mob attacked Cumins' house and killed his daughter and a man named Adam in Pulaski County.
September 28, 1868	A mob killed Crasban Richardson at his home in Conishville.
October 26, 1868	Mob hung Terry Laws and James Ryan at Nicholasville.
December 1868	Two Negroes were shot by the Klan at Sulphur Springs in Union County.
December 1868	Negro was shot at Morganfield Union County.

January 20, 1869	The Klan whipped William Parker in Lincoln County.
January 20, 1869	Albert Bradford was killed by men in disguise in Scott County.
March 12, 1869	The Klan whipped a boy at Stanford.
March 1869	Mr. Roberts was killed at the home of Frank Bournes in Jessamine County.
March 30, 1869	A mob hung George Bratcher on Sugar Creek in Garrard County.
May 29, 1869	A mob hung John Penny at Nevada Mercer County.
June 1869	The Klan whipped Lucien Green.
July 1869	A mob attacked Mr. Ronsey's home and killed three men and one woman.
July 2, 1869	The Klan whipped Mr. Miller.
July 1869	A mob killed Mr. and Mrs. Charles Henderson on Silver Creek in Madison County.
July 17, 1869	A mob hung George Molling.
August 9, 1869	A mob hung James Crowders near Lebanon County.
August 1869	A mob tarred and feathered a citizen in Harrison County.
September 1869	The Klan burned down a colored meeting house in Carol County.
September 1869	The Klan whipped a Negro at John Carmin's farm in Fayette County.

September 1869	A mob raided a Negro cabin and killed John Mosteran, Mr. Cash, and Mr. Coffey.
October 1869	The Klan killed George Rose in Madison County.
October 1869	Mob shoots Mr. Shepherd near Parksville.
November 1869	Klan shot man at Frank Searcy's house in Madison County
November 1869	Mob hanged Mr. Searcy in Richmond.
November 1869	Klan shot Robert Mershon's daughter
November 1869	Mob whipped Pope Hall in Willett Washington County.
December 1869	Mob took two Negroes from jail and hanged one.
December 1869	Mob killed two Negroes while in custody near Mayfield.
December 24, 1869	Klan killed Allen Cooper in Adair County
December 1869	Negro whipped while on Scott's farm in Franklin County.
January 20, 1870	Mob hanged Charles Field in Fayette County.
January 31, 1870	Mob took two men from Springfield jail and hanged them.
February 1870	Klan whipped two Negroes in Madison County.

February 1870	Mob hanged Mr. Simms near Kingston, Madison County.
February 1870	Mob hung up Douglass Rodes and whipped him.
February 18, 1870	Mob hung R.L. Byrom at Richmond.
April 5, 1870	Mob hung Mr. Perry near Lancaster, Garrad County.
April 6, 1870	Mob hung Negro at Crab-Orchard in Lincoln County.
April 1870	Mob attacked Mr. Owen's home and shot and killed Mr. Saunders.
April 11, 1870	Mob shot and hung Mr. Sam Lambert in Mercer County.
April 11, 1870	Mob released five white prisoners from federal officers
April 1870	Mob killed William Hart at Mr. Palmer's house.
May 1870	Mob hanged three men near Gloscow, Warren County.
May 1870	Klan killed John Reman in Adair County.
May 14, 1870	Mob hanged Mr. Pleasanton and Daniel and Willis Parker.
May 14, 1870	Klan robbed Negroes and harassed them.
May 1870	Negro Schoolhouse burned by incendiaries in Christian County.

May 1870	Mob hanged Negro at Greenville, Muhlenburgh.
June 4, 1870	Mob burned colored schoolhouse in Woodford County.
June 1870	Mob attacked jail and killed two men in Whitley County.
August 4, 1870	Riot during elections in Harrodsburg; four persons killed.
August 10, 1870	Mob killed Turpin and Parker at Versilled.
August 1870	Band of men killed Simpson Grubbs in Montgomery County.
September 1870	Mob hanged Frank Timberlake at Flemingburg.
September 1870	Klan shot and killed John Simes and his wife in Hay County.
September 1870	Klan hanged Oliver Williams in Madison County.
October 9, 1870	Klan shot Howard Gilbert in Madison County.
October 1870	Klan drove colored people out of Bald-Knob, Franklin County.
December 6, 1870	Two Negroes shot on Harrison Blaton's farm near Frankfort.
December 18, 1870	Two Negroes killed while in civil custody.
December 1870	Klan murdered Howard Million in Fayette County.

December 12, 1870   John Dickerson driven from home while his daughter was raped.

January 7, 1871   Mob hung Negro named George at Cynthiana, Harrison County.

January 7, 1871   Klan killed Negro near Ashland in Fayette County.

January 17, 1871   Mr. Hall was whipped and shot near Shelby County.

January 14, 1871   Klan killed Negro in Hay County

January 13, 1871   Negro Church and schoolhouse were burned in Scott County.

(Sources include: National Archives Washington, D.C. Records of U.S. Senate 42nd Congress first Session as reported by Herbert Apthekers in *A Documentary History of the Negro People In the United States Vol. 1 & Vol2*; Ralph Gizburg's book *100 Years of Lynchings*; and *Without Sanctuary* with foreword written by Congressman John Lewis.)

APPENDIX B

One Year of Lynching for 1900 in the Democratic South

Name	Date	State
Henry Giveney Ripley	January 9	Tennessee
Roger Giveney Ripley	January 9	Tennessee
Rufus Salter	January 11	South Carolina
Anderson Gause	January 16	Tennessee
William Burts	February 17	South Carolina
James Crosby	March 4	Alabama
George Ratliffe	March 4	North Carolina
Thomas Clayton	March 10	Mississippi
John Bailey	March 18	Georgia
Charles Humphries	March 18	Alabama
George Ritter	March 22	North Carolina
Luis Rice Ripley	March 23	Tennessee
Walter Cotton	March 24	Virginia
Williams Edward	March 27	Mississippi
Allen Brooks	April 3	Georgia
Name Unknown	April 5	Virginia
Moses York	April 16	Mississippi
Henry McAfee	April 19	Mississippi
John Peters	April 20	West Virginia

John Hughley	April 22	Florida
Henry Ratcliff	May 1	Mississippi
George Gordon	May 1	Mississippi
Marshall Jones	May 4	Georgia
Name Unknown	May 7	Mississippi
Name Unknown	May 7	Alabama
William Lee	May 11	West Virginia
Alexander Whitney	May 13	Georgia
William Willis	May 14	Georgia
Name Unknown	May 14	Florida
Name Unknown	May 14	Florida
Henry Harris	May 15	Louisiana
Samuel Hinson	May 16	Mississippi
Name Unknown	May 26	Arkansas
Dago Pete	June 3	Mississippi
W.W. Watts	June 5	Virginia
Simon Adams	June 9	Georgia
Name Unknown	June 10	Florida
Mr. Askew	June 10	Mississippi
Mr. Reese	June 10	Mississippi
John Sanders	June 10	Florida
Senny Jefferson	June 11	Georgia
John Brodie	June 12	Arkansas

Seth Cobb	June 12	Louisiana
Nate Mullins	June 17	Arkansas
S.A. Jenkins	June 17	Arkansas
James Barco	June 20	Florida
Robert Davis	June 21	Florida
Frank Gilmore	June 23	Louisiana
Jack Thomas	June 27	Florida
Jordan Hines	June 27	Georgia
John Roe	July 6	Alabama
Jefferson Henry	July 9	Louisiana
John Jennings	July 12	Georgia
Elijah Clark	July 23	Alabama
Jack Hillsman	July 24	Georgia
Name Unknown	July 25	Louisiana
August Thomas	July 25	Louisiana
Baptiste Filean	July 25	Louisiana
Louis Taylor	July 25	Louisiana
Anna Marbry	July 25	Louisiana
Name Unknown	July 25	Louisiana
Silas Jackson	July 25	Louisiana
Robert Charles	July 26	Louisiana
Jack Betts	August 13	Mississippi
Name Unknown	August 19	Virginia

Name Unknown	August 26	Tennessee
Frank Brown	September 7	Mississippi
Grant Weley	September 8	Georgia
Name Unknown	September 11	North Carolina
Thomas J. Amos	September 11	Louisiana
David Moore	September 14	Mississippi
William Brown	September 14	Mississippi
Charles Elliott	September 21	Louisiana
Nathaniel Bowman	September 21	Louisiana
Isaiah Rollins	September 21	Louisiana
George Beckham	September 21	Louisiana
Winfield Thomas	October 2	Alabama
Mr. Williams	October 8	Tennessee
Wiley Johnson	October 9	Louisiana
Fratur Warfield	October 18	Kentucky
Frank Hardenman	October 19	Georgia
Gloster Barnes	October 23	Mississippi
James Suer	October 24	Georgia
James Calaway	October 24	Georgia
Mr. Abernathy	October 30	Alabama
Name Unknown	November 15	Texas
Name Unknown	November 15	Texas
Name Unknown	November 15	Texas

Daniel Long	December 8	Virginia
Name Unknown	December 19	Mississippi
Mr. Lewis	December 20	Mississippi
Name Unknown	December 21	Arkansas
George Faller	December 28	Georgia

- Sources includes Herbert Aptheker's book, *A Documentary History of the Negro People in the United States Vol. 1 & Vol 2*, Ralph Gizburg's book; *100 Years of Lynchings*, and *Without Sanctuary* with foreword written by congressman John Lewis

APPENDIX C

"The Southern Manifesto"

[From *Congressional Record*, 84th Congress Second Session. Vol. 102, part 4 (March 12, 1956). Washington, D.C.: Governmental Printing Office, 1956. 4459-4460.]

THE DECISION OF THE SUPREME COURT IN THE SCHOOL CASES DECLARATION OF CONSTITUTIONAL PRINCIPLES

Mr. [Walter F.] GEORGE. Mr. President, the increasing gravity of the situation following the decision of the Supreme Court in the so-called segregation cases, and the peculiar stress in sections of the country where this decision has created many difficulties, unknown and unappreciated, perhaps, by many people residing in other parts of the country, have led some Senators and some Members of the House of Representatives to prepare a statement of the position which they have felt and now feel to be imperative.

I now wish to present to the Senate a statement on behalf of 19 Senators, representing 11 States, and 77 House Members, representing a considerable number of States likewise. . . .

DECLARATION OF CONSTITUTIONAL PRINCIPLES

The unwarranted decision of the Supreme Court in the public school cases is now bearing the fruit always produced when men substitute naked power for established law.

The Founding Fathers gave us a Constitution of checks and balances because they realized the inescapable lesson of history that no man or group of men can be safely entrusted with unlimited power. They framed this Constitution with its provisions for change by amendment in order to secure the fundamentals of government against the dangers of temporary popular passion or the personal predilections of public officeholders.

We regard the decisions of the Supreme Court in the school cases as a clear abuse of judicial power. It climaxes a trend in the Federal Judiciary undertaking to legislate, in derogation of the authority of Congress, and to encroach upon the reserved rights of the States and the people.

The original Constitution does not mention education. Neither does the 14th Amendment nor any other amendment. The debates preceding the submission of the 14th Amendment clearly show that there was no intent that it should affect the system of education maintained by the States.

The very Congress which proposed the amendment subsequently provided for segregated schools in the District of Columbia.

When the amendment was adopted in 1868, there were 37 States of the Union. . . .

Every one of the 26 States that had any substantial racial differences among its people, either approved the operation of segregated schools already in existence or subsequently established such schools by action of the same law-making body which considered the 14th Amendment.

As admitted by the Supreme Court in the public school case (*Brown* v. *Board of Education*), the doctrine of separate but equal schools "apparently originated in *Roberts* v. *City of Boston* (1849), upholding school segregation against attack as being violative of a State constitutional guarantee of equality." This constitutional doctrine began in the North, not in the South, and it was followed not only in Massachusetts, but in Connecticut, New York, Illinois, Indiana, Michigan, Minnesota, New Jersey, Ohio, Pennsylvania and other northern states until they, exercising their rights as states through the constitutional processes of local self-government, changed their school systems.

In the case of *Plessy* v. *Ferguson* in 1896 the Supreme Court expressly declared that under the 14th Amendment no person was denied any of his rights if the States provided separate but equal facilities. This decision has been followed in many other cases. It is notable that the Supreme Court, speaking through Chief Justice Taft, a former President of the United States, unanimously declared in 1927 in *Lum* v. *Rice* that the "separate but equal" principle is "within the discretion of the State in regulating its public schools and does not conflict with the 14th Amendment."

This interpretation, restated time and again, became a part of the life of the people of many of the States and confirmed their habits, traditions, and way of life. It is founded on elemental humanity and commonsense, for parents should not be deprived by Government of the right to direct the lives and education of their own children.

Though there has been no constitutional amendment or act of Congress changing this established legal principle almost a century old, the Supreme Court of the United States, with no legal basis for such action, undertook to exercise their naked judicial power and substituted their personal political and social ideas for the established law of the land.

This unwarranted exercise of power by the Court, contrary to the Constitution, is creating chaos and confusion in the States principally affected. It is destroying the amicable relations between the white and Negro races that have been created through 90 years of patient effort by the good people of both races. It has planted hatred and suspicion where there has been heretofore friendship and understanding.

Without regard to the consent of the governed, outside mediators are threatening immediate and revolutionary changes in our public schools systems. If done, this is certain to destroy the system of public education in some of the States.

With the gravest concern for the explosive and dangerous condition created by this decision and inflamed by outside meddlers:

We reaffirm our reliance on the Constitution as the fundamental law of the land.

We decry the Supreme Court's encroachment on the rights reserved to the States and to the people, contrary to established law, and to the Constitution.

We commend the motives of those States which have declared the intention to resist forced integration by any lawful means.

We appeal to the States and people who are not directly affected by these decisions to consider the constitutional principles involved against the time when they too, on issues vital to them may be the victims of judicial encroachment.

Even though we constitute a minority in the present Congress, we have full faith that a majority of the American people believe in the dual system of government which has enabled us to achieve our greatness and will in time demand that the reserved rights of the States and of the people be made secure against judicial usurpation.

We pledge ourselves to use all lawful means to bring about a reversal of this decision which is contrary to the Constitution and to prevent the use of force in its implementation.

In this trying period, as we all seek to right this wrong, we appeal to our people not to be provoked by the agitators and troublemakers invading our States and to scrupulously refrain from disorder and lawless acts.

Appendix D

 ENCYCLOPÆDIA BRITANNICA, INC.

Editorial Offices

November 11, 1994

The Rev. Wayne Perryman
President
Consultants Confidential
P.O. Box 256
Mercer Island, WA 98040

Dear Mr. Perryman:

Thank you for your recent comments concerning treatment in the encyclopaedia of biblical passages relating to Noah, Ham, and Canaan.

The Micropaedia entry "Noah" (3:737:2a), in a discussion of themes that have been traced in Genesis 9:20-27, states that during Noah's drunkenness, his son Ham acted disrespectfully toward him, whereupon Ham was cursed by Noah. As you noted, however, the passage in Genesis states that Noah placed a curse upon Canaan, and not Ham. The *Britannica* entry will be amended in this regard as soon as our revision schedule permits.

The *Britannica* entry also states that the above passage may have been used as a veiled justification for the subjection of the Canaanites by the Israelites. Certainly, most scholars acknowledge this possibility, and we have no plans to delete this information from the entry. Other sources have noted that historically, the passage has been cited--however inappropriately--as evidence in favor of the enslavement or degradation of people of African descent. It is our belief that neither the biblical text in question, nor its treatment in the *Encyclopaedia Britannica*, could be logically used to support such a claim.

Thank you for having taken the time to comment.

Sincerely yours,

Stephen P. Davis
Editorial Division

THOMAS NELSON PUBLISHERS
Nelson Place at Elm Hill Pike. P.O. Box 141000 Nashville. Tenn.. 37214-1000

October 26, 1994

Rev. Wayne Perryman
Consultants Confidential
P.O. Box 256
Mercer Island, WA 98040

Dear Rev. Perryman:

On behalf of our President, Mr. Sam Moore, I want to thank you for your letters and phone calls identifying errors in NELSON'S ILLUSTRATED BIBLE DICTIONARY regarding "the curse of Ham."

I'm grateful that you already know that we are interested in correcting inaccuracies and in demonstrating sensitivity toward the feelings and interests of African Americans, who rightfully object to intentional racism and also to the harmful effects of mistakes that play into its ugly hand. Our interest is grounded in our desire to honor God and help advance His good purposes for all people through our products.

I hope it will please you to know that we are in the process of thoroughly revising NELSON'S ILLUSTRATED BIBLE DICTIONARY and are correcting errors in the specific entries you listed in your letter to Mark Roberts of March 25, 1994. I look forward to sending you a complimentary copy of NELSON'S NEW ILLUSTRATED BIBLE DICTIONARY upon its release, late spring 1995. Also, we are exercising care in our other publishing projects not only to avoid such outright errors, but also to avoid expressions from which some might draw unwarranted and racist inferences.

The original NELSON'S ILLUSTRATED BIBLE DICTIONARY was edited by the late Dr. Herbert Lockyer, Sr., who was apparently unaware of the issues you have raised. Today, with the help of your communications and also of our relationships with an increasing circle of African-American scholars, editors, and writers, we are more able to identify errors and blindspots of perception that need to be corrected and challenged so that our work testifies to the truth in love.

Again, thank you for challenging us to serve all of God's people without offense. We invite you to watch our response to these issues from here on and hope you will be pleased with our sincerity and progress.

Sincerely,

Philip P. Stoner
Vice President
Biblical & Religious Reference Publishing

cc: Hon. Andrew Young, Mr. Sam Moore

≝ ZondervanPublishingHouse

January 20, 1995

Rev. Wayne Perryman, President
Consultants Confidential
P.O. Box 256
Mercer Island, WA 98040

Dear Wayne:

Please excuse the tardiness of my reply to our correspondence and discussions of last October.
However, I believe that I warned you that the next couple of months were exceedingly busy
for me and that it would be some time before I could get back to you with a more official
indication of our decision with regard to the "Curse of Ham" sections in several books that you
called to our attention.

In this more formal way I want to notify you that I have taken steps to make the necessary
corrections, removing the "Curse of Ham" interpretation from the titles that you mentioned,
and revising the text to more faithfully reflect what the Genesis 9 passage actually says.

I went beyond the information that you gave me and, just as I suspected, found several other
titles that also had this interpretation in them. However, these additional titles were simply
earlier editions of the same works that you had mentioned to me. So far as I know, this
completely removes this interpretation from any Zondervan products. The titles that will be
corrected in their next printings are:

Nave's Compact Topical Bible
The Nave's Topical Bible
The NIV Compact Nave's Topical Bible
The Zondervan NIV Nave's Topical Bible
Commentary on the Whole Bible by Matthew Henry, edited by Leslie F. Church
The NIV Matthew Henry Commentary in One Volume, revising editor Gerald W. Peterman.

I trust you understand that most of these titles have a number of months of inventory
remaining in our warehouse, and there are even more books that are in the "pipeline" with
distributors and bookstores around the country. So, it could be a number of months, maybe
even a year or two before the pipeline is completely cleared of the old editions.

But as I indicated above, I am taking steps immediately to make sure that corrections are made
to the appropriate page of each volume so that when we go to the next printing we will be
ready with the corrected text.

Cordially,

Stanley N. Gundry
Vice President and Editor-in-Chief
Book Group

FACT FINDING INVESTIGATIVE SOURCES

Sources Cited in the Text

Aptheker, Herbert. *Documentary History of Negro People in the United States Vol. 2.* New York: Carol Publishers, 1990.

Boyer, Paul S. *The Oxford Companion to United States History.* New York: Oxford University Press, Inc., 2001.

Donald, David Herbert. *Charles Sumner* New York: DA Capo, 1996.

Encyclopedia Britannica, Vol. 9 "Reconstruction" Chicago: IL: 1992.

Franklin, John Hope. *Black Americans.* New York: Time Life Books, 1973.

Franklin, John Hope. *Reconstruction after the Civil War.* New York: McGraw Hill,

Franklin, John Hope and Alfred A. Moss. *From Slavery to Freedom.* New York: McGraw Hill, 1998.

Goodwin, Doris Kearns, *Lyndon Johnson and the American Dream*, New York, St. Martin's Press, 1991

Hall, Kermit L. *The Oxford Companion to the Supreme Court of the United States.* New York: Oxford University Press, Inc., 2005.

Hunt, John Gabriel. *The Inaugural Addresses of the Presidents.* New York: Gramercy Books, 1997.

Lindsey, Howard O. *History of Black America.* New Jersey: Chartwell Books, 1994.

McPherson, James M. *The Abolitionist Legacy: From Reconstruction to the NAACP* Princeton, New Jersey: Princeton University Press, 1975.

Obama, Barack. *Dreams from My Father.* New York: Three Rivers Press, 1995.

Ploski, Harry A. and James Williams. *The Negro Almanac: A Reference Work on the African American Fifth Edition.* Detroit: Gale Research, Inc., 1989.

Schwartz, Bernard. *Statutory History of the United States Civil Rights Part I.* New York: McGraw Hill Book Co., 1970.

Schwartz, Bernard. *Statutory History of United States, Commerce Clearing House: Voting Records on House Bills, 1970.*

Trelease, Allen W. *Reconstruction: The Great Experience.* New York: Harper & Row Publishers, 1971.

Witcover, Jules. *Party of the People: A History of the Democrats.* New York: Random House, 2003.

Wofford, Harris *Of Kennedys & Kings: Making Sense of the Sixties.* Canada: McGraw-Hill, 1980.

Additional Sources

100 Years of Lynchings
Ralph Gizburg

The Abolitionist Sisterhood
Jean Fagan Yellin

The American Nation (textbook)
Prentice Hall

The American Presidents

Grolier Books

America's Constitution: A Biography
Akhil Reed Amar

Black Business in the New South
Walter B. Weare

Black Families in Therapy: A Multisystem Approach
Nancy Boyd Franklin

Black Lies, White Lies
Tony Brown

Black Women in America: An Historical Encyclopedia
Darlene Clark Hine

Booker T. Washington
Jan Gleiter and Kathleen Thompson

At Canaan's Edge
Taylor Branch

The Audacity of Hope
Barack Obama

The Case for Black Reparations
By Boris I. Bittkery

The Causes of the Civil War
Kenneth M. Stamp

The Clash of the Cultures
Joseph A. Raelin

Conspiracy to Destroy Black Boys
Jawanza Kunjufu

Copperheads: The Rise and Fall of Lincoln's Opponent in the North
Jennifer L. Weber

A Death in the Delta: The Story of Emmett Till
Stephen J. Whitfield

Disuniting of America
Arthur M. Schlesinger Jr

The Fabulous Democrats
David L. Cohn

George Washington Carver: An American Biography
Rackham Holt

The Myth of Separation
David Barton

The Negro Family in the United States
Frazier E. Franklin

Raising Black Children
Alvin F. Poussaint and James P. Comer

The Republicans: A History of Their Party
Malcolm Moos

The Scottsboro Boys
James Haskins

Slavery and the Making of America
James Oliver Horton and Lois E. Horton

The Struggle for Equality
James McPherson

The Way of the Bootstrapper
Floyd Flake

Why We Can't Wait
Rev. Dr. Martin Luther King

Without Sanctuary
Leon F. Litwack (Foreword by Congressman John Lewis)

News Media Sources & Film Documentaries

PBS Special: The Rise & Fall of Jim Crow, Parts 1,2,3 &4

PBS Special: Reconstruction: The Second Civil War, Part 1 & 2

PBS Special: Citizen King

PBS Special: Abraham & Mary Lincoln: A House Divided, Part 1, 2, &3

David Barton: Justice at the Gate Reconciliation

History Channel: Voices of Civil Rights

FDR: A Presidency Revealed, Part 1 &2

United States Congress & Government Records

- National Archives Washington D.C. Records of U.S. Senate 42nd Congress first Session

- Joint Select Committee to Inquire into Conditions of Affairs in the Late Insurrectionary States *Senate Report No. 579* in the 48th Congress.

- *Transcripts* of Congressional Debates on Civil Rights Cases

- *Congressional Record*, 84th Congress Second Session. Vol. 102, part 4 (March 12, 1956).

- New Orleans Comprehensive Emergency Preparedness Plan

The 13th Amendment

Fernando Wood's Comments
> Pages 44, 46   *Statutory History of the Untied States*

James Wilson's Comments
> Page 29, 35   *Statutory History of the Untied States*

1866 Civil Rights Acts

Willard Saulsbury's Comments
> Page 113   *Statutory History of the Untied States*

Reverdy Johnson's Comments
> Page 119   *Statutory History of the Untied States*

William Fessenden's Comments
> Page 119   *Statutory History of the Untied States*

Martin Thayer's Comments
> Pages 130-131   *Statutory History of the Untied States*

Michael Kerr's Comments
> Pages 135-136   *Statutory History of the Untied States*

The First Reconstruction Act of 1867

Ben Tillman's Comments
> Page 427   The *American Nation*

The 14th Amendment

Andrew Rogers' Comments
> Page 246   *Statutory History of the Untied States*

The 15th Amendment

William Stewart's Comments
> Page 375   *Statutory History of the Untied States*

Garrett Davis Comments
  Page 382   *Statutory History of the Untied States*

Thomas Hendrick's Comments
  Page 403   *Statutory History of the Untied States*

James Patterson's Comments
  Pages 406-407   *Statutory History of the Untied States*

The Enforcement Act of 1870

James Bayard's Comments
  Page 511   *Statutory History of the Untied States*

William Stewart's Comments
  Pages 516-519   *Statutory History of the Untied States*

The Force Act of 1871

Charles Eldredge's Comments
  Pages 559, 561+   *Statutory History of the Untied States*

John Churchill's Comments
  Pages 565-566   *Statutory History of the Untied States*

Ku Klux Klan Act of 1871

William Stoughton's Comments
  Pages 599-605   *Statutory History of the Untied States*

George Morgan's Comments
  Pages 607-608   *Statutory History of the Untied States*

George McKee's Comments
  Pages 611-612   *Statutory History of the Untied States*

Civil Rights Act of 1875

Frederick Frelinguhuysen Comments
  Page 666   *Statutory History of the Untied States*

William Saulsbury's Comments
    Pages 697-698   *Statutory History of the Untied States*

Repeal Act of 1894

George Hoar's Comments
    Pages 827, 831-832 *Statutory History of the Untied States*

1957 Civil Rights Act

William Winstead's Comments
    Page 878   *Statutory History of the Untied States*

Cliffor Case's Comments
    Page 885   *Statutory History of the Untied States*

William Colmer's Comments
    Page 920   *Statutory History of the Untied States*

Richard Russell's Comments
    Pages 926-927, 932
                        Statutory History of the Untied States

1960 Civil Rights Act

Ray Madden's Comments
    Page 956   *Statutory History of the Untied States*

Overton Brooks' Comments
    Page 964   *Statutory History of the Untied States*

William McColloch's Comments
    Page 965   *Statutory History of the Untied States*

1964 Civil Rights Act

Dr. Martin Luther King's Comments
    Pages 5-6   *Why We Can't Wait*

Bernard Schwartz's Comments
    Page 1017   *Statutory History of the Untied States*

President Kennedy's Message
    Page 1055   *Statutory History of the Untied States*

Emmanuel Celler's Comments
    Page 1099   *Statutory History of the Untied States*

Thomas Abernethy's Comments
    Page 1128   *Statutory History of the Untied States*

Donald Matthews's Comments
    Page 1135   *Statutory History of the Untied States*

Sam Ervin's Comments
    Page 1307   *Statutory History of the Untied States*

Robert Byrd's Comments
    Page 1341   *Statutory History of the Untied States*

Olin Johnston's Comments
    Page 1404   *Statutory History of the Untied States*

Howard Smith's Comments
    Page 1421   *Statutory History of the Untied States*

William McCullough's Comments
    Page 1112   *Statutory History of the Untied States*

Everett Dirksen's Comments
    Page 1141   *Statutory History of the Untied States*

John Sparkman's Comments
    Pages 1151-53   *Statutory History of the Untied States*

1965 Voting Rights Act

President Johnson's Address
    Page 1506   *Statutory History of the Untied States*

Sam Ervin's Comments
   Page 1512   *Statutory History of the Untied States*

Everett Dirksen's Comments
   Page 1512   *Statutory History of the Untied States*

Herman Talmadge's Comments
   Page 1542   *Statutory History of the Untied States*

Jacob Javit's Comments
   Page 1575   *Statutory History of the Untied States*

1968 Civil Rights Act

Lawrence Fountain's Comments
   Page 1668   *Statutory History of the Untied States*

Everett Dirksen's Comments
   Page 1684   *Statutory History of the Untied States*

Sam Ervin's Comments
   Page 1686   *Statutory History of the Untied States*

John Stennis' Comments
   Page 1757   *Statutory History of the Untied States*